MW01675613

WHEN THE MERRY-GO-ROUND STOPS

BY LEE PETERSON

BRUNSWICK PRESS
P.O. Box 2244
Cathedral City,CA. 92235
USA

Library of Congress catalog card number

ISBN 1-888521-18-X

First Edition

Brunswick Press
P.O. Box 2244
Cathedral City, CA. 92235

Acknowledgment

I want to thank my entire family and many wonderful friends who made this book possible by being in it, and giving me encouragement throughout the writing.

Thank you Harvey and Lori for making my life so interesting.

A special "Thank You" to my dear Bumper who was my assistant and had faith in me, knowing I could write a book.

Having lived with two very ill heart patients for many years, I wanted to write my story so that people who are in the same situation will know they are not alone.

to Marilyn —
Enjoy the Ride —
With Love,
Lee Peterson

PART I

THE CATERPILLAR

BIG DECISION

I'm going to barber school!

It all started the end of 1978 when my husband Bumper had a serious heart attack. We found out he had been having silent heart attacks and his heart was severely damaged. He was only in his 30's and were told that he would have to retire.

He could no longer work and I hadn't been working, and the options were few in the small town of Zimmerman, Minnesota, where Jobs there were scarce and the pay was next to nothing.

We had four children so it was a scary time for us. Not only did Bumper have a bad heart, but also our daughter Sonja, in high school, had been born with a congenital heart defect. Knowing that I now had two serious heart patients and no job, I would have to come up with something fast!

One day Bumper and I went to the nearby town of Anoka for a haircut because we couldn't afford a violin for him and he refused to wear a dog collar. The barber agreed with me that the follically challenged man, with hair hanging over his ears, was in need of his service.

I noticed how many heads of hair could be cut in a short time, listened to them sling the bull, and I liked what I saw. When we got into the car, my words were, "I CAN DO THAT, I'M GOING TO BARBER SCHOOL!"

With no talent for any specialized job, driving daily to Minneapolis 35 miles away, would not be a good idea unless it was to better myself. Bumper agreed that barber school might just work out for me.

Our small town did have a barber, but being in his 80's, he was retiring in a few months. The older men who wanted short haircuts went to him. He knew only one style of haircut so there was definitely need for another barber.

As I sat in the shop the experience of Pastor Tom, our new clergyman, came to mind. He had gone to the barber expecting a 70's cut, which meant leaving some hair covering the ears. What he got was a cut next to bald. His wife told me that he came home and cried. The first Sunday at his new church he was embarrassed and I felt sorry for him. That was his first and last visit to our old barber.

That night at dinner I told my four children I was going to barber school and that they would all have to pitch in and help Bumper as much as possible. Sonja, because of her heart problem, would get out of any hard work. Bumper would do most of the cooking, and the other three would help with everything else.

After Christmas, I called the barber school and made an appointment for an interview. Knowing what was coming Bumper made a deal with a friend of his, who raised rabbits, to buy a freezer full at a good price. He then read books on how to cook the little critters. The only other things he knew how to cook were roast beef and oatmeal and I feared that would be our menu for the next nine months while I was in school.

The next week I drove to Molar Barber School on 14th and Nicollet in downtown Minneapolis. The school itself looked nice, but the surrounding area needed some clean up work.

Entering the building, I encountered the head of the school, a man named Don. When he found out I was planning to become a barber in a small town, especially the one I lived in, he tried somewhat to discourage me. I think he knew that a woman would have a hard time in a small town, as in those days, men didn't think a woman had any business in the male world of barbering. There were girls in the school, but all of them planned on working in the big cities, which is a whole different ball game than small town U.S.A.

Don told me that at the time, I was the oldest woman ever to go to Molar Barber School, which was the biggest one, and the first one in the state of Minnesota. He was thinking that my age wouldn't help me either, but in my 40's, I certainly wasn't old! I was going to go to Barber School with or without his blessings.

Don thought that I must have had a lifelong dream of becoming a barber, but when I informed him it hadn't crossed my mind until a week ago, he sat and stared at me. While he was pondering what I had just told him I asked him if embalmers loved getting people ready for viewing? I didn't think so. I said, they were in it for the money. I explained that was why I chose to be a barber, also, to make money in a town with no barber!

The school accepted me on the spot, but I think anyone would be if they had all the financing in the palm of their hand, which I had because my brother-in-law and sister had told me they would pay for my schooling. Like everything else it came down to money!

Getting home that day, I let the family know I was going to start school January 30, 1979, and they were all supportive and happy for me. A lot of fear of the unknown was gone, and now I would be busy learning how to make a living.

ROAD TO SCHOOL

Getting to the school each day made my nine months of training a grueling experience. At 4:00 a.m. every morning a man from a neighboring town picked me up in the town where I lived. He let me off on Washington Avenue in Minneapolis in front of a bar called Archie's Bunker. Sometimes it was a long wait for the bus, and standing there in that cold, dark, windy, forlorn spot, I would let my mind run to places where I didn't want to be. I would think, "what a perfect place for a murder, but I hope it's not mine." After boarding the bus, I would barely start to thaw out, when I had to get off to change to a bus going down Nicollet Avenue to the school.

Because of my unique transportation arrangement, I arrived at the school almost an hour early so I would go to a seedy little diner across the street every morning. There I met hookers who had finished their nights work. After a while they began to speak to me knowing I was no threat to them. Candy, who usually worked from early afternoon until early morning, seemed so happy with her job. Even though I was having many problems, I counted my blessings that I wasn't in her shoes. Soon, after she arrived at the dinner, her guy, who I assumed was her pimp, would pick her up. The waitress in the dive was a wonderful character herself, so it was an interesting way to start the day.

Coming home was much easier because I needed only to get a bus to the downtown area and walk to the Federal Building where a man from Zimmerman would pick me up and give me a ride home.

BARBER SCHOOL

School was a lot of fun. Before the week was over, the students, who were all in there twenties, were calling me MOM. The first couple of months were spent in the classroom learning the trade through lectures, reading, and having tests. I knew it would become more interesting when we could start working on the floor. I think the students, who truly liked working with hair, found this part to be fun but I was just doing it because I had to.

Finally, the day came when we each got our own stations on the floor. At that point, Barber School changed for the better.

The Rookies all started on what some may call the "undesirables", but I think of them as the characters and the core of the school so I rather enjoyed them.

Street people were the regulars and my very first customer was truly a street bum. Street people came in to get a shave and a haircut, to get free coffee, or to get out of the weather, or sometimes just to relax.

I washed and cut Dutch's hair, (my first patron) and found him to be very nice, though a bit dirty. I was still too new to give a shave, but that would come later. Dutch stuck with me throughout my novice time. Dutch and his friends were transients who lived under bridges in good weather and shelters, or where ever, the rest of the time. My heart went out to that old guy who was not as old as he looked. The more I got to know Dutch I began to believe that he really wouldn't change that way of life for any other. I hate to think that some people can enjoy a life like that, but he was one of them.

A few weeks later Dutch came back, and this time, I did my very first shave with a straightedge razor. I was terrified but he was as cool as a cucumber. Can you imagine anyone coming at you whose using a razor for the first time? Of course, he had imbibed in some form of tranquilizer, such as wine or liquid sterno, so given those maybe I would have been calm too. I didn't really believe anyone ever drank liquid sterno until I met Dutch. If anything had alcohol in it, he would drink it!

Scared out of my wits that I might cut poor Dutch, I applied the hot towel to his face, and tried to hide the fear in my voice. When the towel came off, I was terrified, because if I were to cut him, an ambulance might have to come and he would be taken, free of charge to the hospital. If he died from being cut in the throat it would be my fault. I needed to calm down and get a little confidence, but that was very hard to do. While shaving him I had a problem with his bad breath and body odor. It seemed he hadn't brushed his teeth for years, and he also hadn't had a bath, but the breath was the biggest problem. Shaving his face was easy, but the next step was to shave his neck and throat. During the shave I didn't even talk to him because I had to concentrate on all they had taught me. When I finished the shave and wrapped the hot towels on his face I was proud of my accomplishment. I was relieved that Dutch was alive and he probably was too, but he had shown no fear throughout the ordeal.

During my time at the school I had many customers that were interesting, but another one that will always be remembered is a young man that came to my chair with big bites all over his arms. I asked him what had happened. He said, "I was playing with my pet." Before I could ask him anything about his pet, he said, "Be careful of my scalp, because the stitches are still there." Gently combing his hair, I saw a HUGE bite, almost surrounding his entire head. I asked him what kind of pet he had and from then on I was in a state of shock. "I have a pet snake and I was playing with him, but when I saw him swelling up, I should have stopped playing." I asked him to explain all this. " Snakes swell up noticeably when they are mad, but I still thought he was playing with me. I think he was playing when he bit my arms, but then he went for my head, and I knew he was no longer playing." I wondered if this guy could be for real? I told him he should write a best seller on HOW SNAKES PLAY!

Luckily for him, some brave friend who had been there, pulled his head away from the snake and called an ambulance. I'm surprised that he knew anyone who would come and visit him with a big boa constrictor in the apartment. I thought they would always squeeze a person to death before eating you but maybe when they are playing they do the opposite. He told me he still had the snake, and would keep it, because it was his pet. I wouldn't live next door to or even in the same vicinity, as someone with such a pet. I never could pin him down to exactly how snakes play. Do they roll over and play dead, and then wake up and bite? Do you kiss him on the mouth and play, MISS THE BITE? I really wanted to know the answers, but I don't think he knew, and I also felt he didn't know enough about this sort of pet to have one. I've always wondered if that snake charmer is still alive. I will never know. Maybe he became snake food.

Between customers, we used to watch the hookers from the window, and count how many times they would get into the cars that had stopped for them. I didn't want the students to know that some of the girls were familiar to me from breakfast at the diner so I kept my higher education to myself.

Next to the diner across the street was a dilapidated little grocery store where we would run to get something for lunch or snacks. I wanted cough syrup one day, but they had nothing in the whole store with any alcohol in it. They were sold out. I guess Dutch and his friends had shopped there.

Graduation day was approaching and it was an exciting time for my family. Soon the kids could eat something other than rabbit. They fully believed this whole time that they were eating chicken, because at one time Sonja had owned a pet rabbit, and when it started eating furniture, shoes, and everything else, we gave it to a rabbit farm. We knew she would not eat a Rabbit. Many years later when I told her she had been eating rabbit, she was appalled. She said she would never eat it again, but was not mad at us for not telling her. The big day finally came, November 5, 1979 and I was a Barber apprentice. I had made it!

THE SHOP

In those days, you had to be an apprentice for over a year before you could become a master Barber. Since the old guy had retired, there was no barber in my small town.

I started my apprenticeship in a shop in a nearby town, where the owner had no great love for women, and I had no great love for him. I think it was mutual dislike from the first day I worked there. After a few months I decided I had absolutely had enough of that, and was going to own my own shop while I was still an apprentice. It is legal to OWN one, but only a Master Barber can MANAGE one. Somehow, I would find a retired Barber that didn't need to make much money, and one that I could trust, although, I didn't know of one. Where there's a will, there has to be a way! Knowing I would find some solution, I started buying things for my shop. Harvey, my brother-in-law (my sister Lori's husband), said to me, "Get what you need and have the bills sent to me." Not many are fortunate enough to have someone like that behind them, but I sure was!

A cabinetmaker friend of ours made 14ft, solid oak back bars, with two sinks for me. From Barber supply, I ordered the biggest Barber Pole, and everything else I would need. I even found an old till! Things were going great guns except for one small detail, no MASTER BARBER!

An old couple that I knew had a lifelong friend named Melvin, who was a retired barber, that they thought might help me. When I called him, I found out that he was the most lovable, wonderful guy in the world. Sure! He would help me out.

When I bought two old barber chairs from Molar School, I had no idea how difficult it would be to move those chairs. I arranged for two guys with a pick up truck to move them but that wasn't enough! Barber Chairs probably weigh more than 300 pounds each, but that wasn't the problem. These can't be tipped up or even turned wrong because the hydraulic fluid will come out. It took a lot of the biggest students, and my two friends, to get those chairs onto the truck.

When we got back to Zimmerman one of the guys really used his head. He went to the hardware store and borrowed a forklift, which proved to be an easy way to get the chairs into the shop.

I rented a cute little spot on Main Street, with a big bay window, so I could watch all the excitement of Main Street. It had a little back room, which I used for my other business, which was a dry cleaning pick up and drop off service. I had it looking like an old fashioned, quaint, men's barber shop.

When opening day finally came, I was proud of that little shop! Just a few doors down the alley behind my shop was the ambulance barn, so the ambulance crew found a new home. I put in a table, chairs, cards, backgammon game and the coffee pot was kept on for anyone coming through the door.

A woman named Ray was a major part of our ambulance EMT (Emergency Medical Technician) unit and she became my best buddy. We started playing backgammon every day, and after one year, I was minus 1000, but I knew that I would get back to zero at some point. She was just having a lucky streak, but with my knowledge, skills, and know how of the game, the law of averages had to run out and her luck would change!

Most of the crew hung out there, and it was wonderful! I was teased because they said I was the only barber in the world with my own ambulance crew standing by! They played cards, or just 'slung the bull,' which was one of the reasons I picked barber school in the first place.

I had some very loyal customers, but of course, there were some that would never come to a woman barber, but they would let Melvin cut their hair. Everyone loved Melvin! He was a good man, but sometimes would have one drink too many, and one day, he came to work much too hung over to do anything, so he slept in the chair in the back room. What the heck, he was there! That was what the law required, and besides, he was the manager!

Not long after we opened, we had the IRS come into the shop to audit our books. I didn't know they made house calls! I kicked them out. Bumper and Melvin told me that was a stupid thing to do. Why would they hassle a small barbershop, that hadn't even been open long enough to make money. Why would those guys drive all the way out from St. Paul? I was mad! The next day they came back and Melvin had to get the books for them. I thought that was really stupid, all the money these guys were making, just to run out to our little shop. They looked at the books for several days, which was not too brilliant because in the short time we were in business the books weren't that complicated to do, but then, they did work for the government!

We found out later that Melvin's ex-wife thought he was making a whole pile of money in his new adventure and wanted to get him into trouble. It didn't work for her but it sure scared the life out of both of us.

One loyal and wonderful customer was Mertin who came every week for a haircut. Customers like that were pure gold!

When my apprenticeship was over, Melvin continued to work on Saturdays just because he wanted to. He would also keep the shop open when Bumper had medical appointments, so Melvin became my crutch. When my mother became sick and died of cancer, Melvin was there to run things.

Bumper had just gotten out of the hospital the day before my mother's funeral, so mother-in-law brought him to church after the service, to see all the relatives.

Randy had graduated, and was attending college in Duluth, Sonja was at Hamline University in St. Paul, and Jon was going to Anoka Tech to be a mechanic, but was living at home. Heidi was now in high school.

SONJA

The doctors knew something was wrong with Sonja's heart minutes after she was born at Princeton Minnesota Hospital in 1960.

She was sent to the University Hospital in Minneapolis for diagnosis, but they did not have the medical knowledge or equipment to find rare abnormalities in her heart at that time. She was diagnosed as having a hole in her heart but nothing could be done at that time.

As a child she would tire easily and her lips and fingers would turn blue. She wouldn't have to take gym or run like the other kids, but that was OK, if she was going to be all right.

She went to the University Hospital for checkups on a regular basis. They thought she was functioning ok, so they didn't want to do surgery. Modern equipment was just around the corner. She was eventually diagnosed as having a hole in her heart and that her heart was upside down and backwards so they didn't want to do surgery at all.

The doctors didn't know what a complete rarity they had in her and we are all glad of that, because had we known the real problem, those growing up years would have been much more frightening and frantic than they were.

When she was eighteen she had to leave the Children's Clinic. We suggested that she go to Ron's doctor at North Memorial Hospital for another opinion of her heart problem.

Dr. Azzam was a lifesaver at that point. Good medical

equipment and technology was coming in fast, and he had access to all of it. He put her in the hospital and really tested her to see what the problem was.

\He found out exactly what the problem was! She was born with three chambers to her heart instead of four. It wasn't exactly upside down and backwards like they had thought; it just appeared that way, because nothing was in the right spot due to the one missing ventricle. How she had stayed alive all those years was a complete mystery to this wonderful man.

Now that we knew the real problem and the severity of it, we were all glad we hadn't known it when she was young, because it couldn't have been corrected and even now they didn't know what to do about it! Fear set in for all of us at that point.

Dr. Azzam assured us that with all the knowledge and technology available, they would find a way to fix her heart, so for now; she should just take it easier than she had in the past.

When I went to see her in her hospital room, she was very down, which is not like her. She said, "I will have to change my lifestyle." I couldn't bear to see her like this, so I said, "So, if you break a leg you have to change your lifestyle, all this means is that you will be doing less than you were before, no big deal." I also said, "This is the biggest blessing we have had so far, because I think this doctor's right and he will figure out what can be done for you, so quit feeling sorry for yourself and count your blessings." You hate to get after a child lying in a hospital bed, but at that point tough love worked.

She continued going to college and leading as normal a life as possible. She was happy and very constructive.

It was good for both her and Bumper; because now they knew they were both real medical wonders. I never saw either of them down after that.

In 1983, Dr. Azzam took Sonja's case to a big medical convention held in Switzerland, where doctors came from all over the world.

He called her in when he got back and told her that all the doctors had gotten together and figured out what to do for her. There was a surgery that should make her normal.

Dr. Azzam referred her back to the University of Minnesota to see Dr. Wang, who would be the very best doctor for her rare problem. She loved Dr. Wang from the first visit and had all the faith in the world in that fine man. She called us right after the visit and told us about the operation they could do and also that she would not live another ten years without having it done. We were so happy!

Then Sonja said to me, "Will it bother Dad if I get this surgery?" At that point, I was trying to keep from crying and told her, "Absolutely Not! Go for it! Nothing would make everyone happier." There she was, in her own miserable condition, worrying if Bumper could take the strain of her going into surgery. She thought the worry would kill him! I knew she should not have thought about that but she made me very proud to be her mother. She is the kindest person in the world and I don't say that just because I'm her mother!

A few more weeks to wait and maybe Sonja would be a normal person with an almost normal heart.

God really is always with us. What if we hadn't gotten her to Bumper's doctor? What if they figured she would be OK? Yes, Count our many blessings.

PETS

When the kids were in grade school I got this huge white dog, a mixture of shepherd, husky and St. Bernard. Best dog in the whole world. When I got her I thought she was retarded because, stupid me, I thought all dogs lifted their leg and this one didn't. I also thought she was a He. I hadn't married Bumper yet so he didn't know how little I knew about animals. When my He dog, named Sam, had puppies at age 8, I thought she was sick and took her to the vet. She was about 140 pounds so pregnancy didn't show on her. Bumper, now my husband, didn't know it either because he wasn't home when she got sick. When the vet said she was having puppies it was a true shock to everyone. She delivered 4 puppies, two pure white, one mixed color and one dark one that died, even though Bumper stayed up all night trying to breathe life into him. When they were tiny we had to paint the white ones with food color to see them in the snow. We gave away two of them and kept one male. It was true this time because Bumper knows boy dogs. His name was Lars and he looked like mama but didn't have as many brains as Sam. Those dogs were the love of the whole family. Heidi, maybe in fourth grade, wanted a cat so badly that she talked "cat hating Bumper" into getting me one for Mother's Day. He actually went to someone's barn and picked out a 6 weeks old black kitten. When they returned I opened up a box and there was Bandit!

Bandit was about the size of my hand and had more guts than most animals. He stood in the middle of a big broiler pan, which was the dogs feeding dish and hissed at those two large beasts looking at him. That showed me that my cat had courage! The dogs looked at the tiny little thing, felt sorry for him and soon became his adopted parents. That first night with us Bandit slept curled up in Sam's paws. They loved that cat!

Bumper, definitely not a cat lover, said we could keep the cat until it was grown, then out it would go. The kids and I didn't worry much about that threat because Bumper is really a pussy cat, and, if the dogs loved him that quickly, we knew it would rub off on the cat hater. It did!

When Bandit was almost full grown, I said to Bumper, "I suppose we have to get rid of him soon." He said, "No, he can stay longer." Of course, by this time the cat was also one of Bumper's loves and I knew he would never get rid of his little black cat. In fact, if he had to pick between the cat or me, it would have been a toss up, and I may not have gotten the blue ribbon!

Bandit was the leader of the pack and it was hard to believe the three of them could actually understand each other, but they did. Sam and Lars were taught never to take food off the table, although they were tall enough. Bandit must have told them that anything on the floor was fair game, so the black leader would get on the table or counter and push any food off to his pure white buddies, who were standing and waiting for whatever would fall. Bandit ate no people food because he didn't like it, but he sure took care of his best friends. We left food out purposely to watch this charade and it was the cutest thing we have ever seen. The three were inseparable.

We had Sam put to sleep when she was 12 and that was a hard thing to do. When Sam died, Lars took over Sam's patrol of the neighbors' homes and got a whole lot smarter. Lars and Bandit were the best buddies in the world.

One day, our neighbor called and said, "Come over, you have to see this." Lars and Bandit were each lying on the ground, feet facing each other, and a brave field mouse was running back and forth from Lars 's paws to bandits paws, and back again and again and again. This was the funniest sight in the world. The field mouse should have died of a heart attack, but it seemed he was having fun making

Lars and Bandit look like Dumb and Dumber. You would think any cat would love to kill a mouse but not Bandit, he had learned not to kill things from the dogs.

During winter, the two huge dogs were in the house a lot, so our small home with one bathroom and three tiny bedrooms, was very crowded, but we survived well. That is what you call a close family.

Lars didn't live as long as Sam and when she got sick and died, it devastated Bandit. He would spend all day looking for his best buddy. Bumper and I watched and cried. We would have to do something for the poor cat.

A few weeks later Sonja called and said the Humane Society was looking for a home for a Lhasa Apso that had been taken away from a breeding farm because it had been abused there. If we were interested, the woman from the Humane Society wanted to come out and see us, because she wanted to check out the home before they would give this dog to anyone.

We had no idea what a Lhasa was but said, "Sure we would love to have him." Bandit needed another friend.

When the women came out she asked us a lot of questions. We told her that Bumper was disabled from his heart condition so he would be home all the time with the dog. We had to promise not to have him "fixed" because of his championship bloodline (with papers) to prove his pedigree. We got our new pet.

Bandit didn't think much of him, but he allowed him to use his house.

ARIZONA

My folks had a beautiful home in Arizona bought for them by Harvey and Lori. After mom died Grandpa went back there for three months each winter. Grandpa would have been just as happy in an old run down shack because he hadn't been a very happy person since mother died. Grandpa was always a loving father and cared about his looks, but after her death, he was never the same person. He was lost without her.

The shop was closed the first two weeks in January every year. Lori told me that she would get me an airline ticket and I could accompany Grandpa to Arizona because he didn't travel well by himself. She said some work needed to be done on the house, so she would also get a ticket for Bumper or our son Jon, who had two weeks off from school, to go with me to fix up the place while I cleaned it and got grandpa settled in. She knew I would be busy but I could bathe in the sun, swim in the pool and relax the rest of the time.

Taking Bumper to Arizona to do some work was a dumb idea because he wasn't good at fixing anything when he was healthy, so he wouldn't be much help. Bumper was afraid to fly and being around my father for two weeks would not be good for anyone's blood pressure. We decided he would stay home since Heidi was there to help him after school and the neighbors would be around.

Jon loves to travel, but spending two weeks with my sister's father? And fixing up the place? After Lori said she would get us a rental car, he thought maybe we might be able to have a good time.

Grandpa hates all kinds of work, so he didn't do any. A cleaning lady came every week but he really needed one to come in about twice a day.

Grandpa had only one hobby and that was smoking, preferably a pipe. He filled it to overflowing and made a mess with tobacco falling all over the place. He lit it, took a few puffs and banged it upside down so all the tobacco fell out. Once in a while he would hit the ashtray. Then, he would fill it, puffed, banged it out and started over again. He followed that same routine all day long unless he was smoking a cigarette and would use his pants' cuff for an ashtray. When I harped at him about this terrible habit, he had a bad hearing problem.

I guess he did have one other habit and that was to sit in the house and feel sorry for himself, expecting everyone else to sit with him and feel sorry for him too. I did not have time for that!

Before we left for Arizona, Jon was finally excited about going because he knew he would come back with a beautiful tan and with his husky build and blond hair, he figured the girls would really flock to him.

Bumper was sad that I would be gone and Heidi was kind of mad that she would be left to take care of Bumper because she knew she would be doing everything. I was, by this time, glad to be going to a warm climate, but knew the mess I would have on my return. Heidi and Bumper? What a pair!

We left early the morning of our departure because Grandpa, called Grumps by Jon, was worried about getting to the airport on time. We stopped for breakfast along the way and still got there two hours early. Jon was already getting mad at Grumps and we hadn't even left yet!

Landing in Phoenix, most of Grandpa's food from the flight had landed on his clothes, so he looked normal. On our way to pick up the rental car, Grumps saw BUDGET CAR RENTAL and he said we should go there. I said, "No, we are going to Hertz". He had a fit and said it would be much cheaper getting a budget one. Why did he care? He wasn't paying for it! He said, "You don't know what you are doing." I said, " Yes, I do." He said, "I don't think you do." That was our first few minutes in the Sunbelt!

Jon drove the car and Grumps wanted to give directions, but a totally different way than Hertz had given us. With Grandpa hollering and me trying to give him the right directions from Hertz, Jon accidentally made a wrong turn where Grumps said to turn. That little venture took us one and a half hours and we missed every stoplight getting to his place. The pouring rain and cloudy dark skies, were not what we had expected and made the drive even worse.

A few days later we decided to test the route so we took the same trip, again through the rain and the trip took us twenty minutes via the Hertz route. Grumps still insisted his way was better because there wasn't so much traffic!

When we arrived at the house everything was in good shape except for a big hole in the roof. It's a good thing it was raining or we may have missed the big mess in the living room. Grumps wanted the roof fixed that very minute but Jon put down pans and said he would take care of it when the rain stopped. Not only was it raining, it was cold, which was out of the ordinary for a fun filled vacation in the sun. Tomorrow it would be sunny for sure and Jon and I would get our tans that Lori had promised us.

Grumps didn't sleep much that night, he sat up worrying about how much the roof was going to cost him. He was sure that Jon knew nothing about fixing anything. He didn't think Lori would be happy if he charged it to her, so that kept him busy the first night. I got up and told Gramps not to worry because, 1-maybe Jon could fix it. 2-If Jon couldn't fix it we would send the bill to Lori. 3- He could fix it himself, which he COULD afford and still wouldn't come close to starving to death. He didn't worry much about 1 and 2 after that, but he sure did worry about number 3!

I woke up early in the morning to the banging of the pipes, but not the Scottish pipes of Scotland. No, it was the banging of Grumps' pipe. By now he wanted coffee, but he sure wouldn't make it himself with me there! I ran for the window to check out the beautiful day we would have, but it was RAINING!

Grumps was worried how Jon would get on the roof with no ladder and how he would get up in the rain, but Jon was already climbing down. He had discovered where the problem was, Jon assured Grumps he could fix the roof, but would rather wait for the rain to stop. Being a flat roof it only needed hot tar, more shingles and some rock. No big deal! Grumps still argued that he wanted it done right then and there, but Jon told him you could not pour hot tar in the rain.

All Grumps had to worry about now was when it would stop raining and how much it would cost him. While he sat and worried, I washed clothes, cleaned and went grocery shopping. Jon went with me because Grumps didn't need any help worrying. He could do that very well by himself!

I have never in my life seen one human being that could sit and do NOTHING the whole day. He probably blinked, did go to the bathroom and ate. That was it for the first day, except to worry! He did brag about all the work he had done.

Grumps had always said there was nothing to do in the retirement community where he lived. Grandma always found things to do. Jon and I took him to the Clubhouse to see what was happening. The Clubhouse was filled with retired people going to various clubs; lapidary, sewing, woodworking, exercising and that was only the IN-DOOR things. When it was not raining, they had lawn bowling, shuffleboard, swimming, hot tub and golfing. How can there be nothing to do? Jon told him he should join the

Minnesota Club where everyone would be from his own state. Grumps got mad. Jon added, "They probably are real expensive to join, maybe cost a couple of bucks each month." In Grumps' mind, that would surely put him right in the "poor house".

Grumps had an Aunt that was in her late 80's and Grandpa was close to 80 himself. She lived not very far from Grumps. We invited her to spend the day with us and after checking her date book, she found a free day, so she drove over. Grumps didn't care much for Alma because she made him clean up and get off his butt. She was good for him!

We all went to lunch and then for a drive. Alma was wishing Jon had brought his truck so they could go 4 wheeling out in the desert and up into the mountains. Grumps thought Alma ran around too much, when she should be saving her money for her old age! He also doesn't like living in a community with a bunch of OLD people!

The banging of the pipes woke me the next morning along with the sound of rain. We went to the store. Grumps went with us and the trip took six hours. Picking up Alma, we headed up the mountain to Tortilla Flats, which was a store, cafe and a bunch of poorly built buildings made to look like a town. Any mother that hasn't taken a trip up curvy mountain roads with her son driving, has not lived and I really didn't think I would! He enjoyed seeing how fast the car could go around curves with no guardrails. That macho mouseketeer had me so scared that I could not move or speak! Jon wanted to go further up the mountain to Roosevelt Dam, but the gravel roads were closed because of rain. Thank God! Jon said, "We'll go up there some day when it's not raining." Under my breath I said, " In your dreams!" The trip down wasn't much better and I knew I would have to find a bathroom soon, but not until we were down. Getting down and still being alive was the most important thing. Alma never seemed to be scared and Grumps just sat and smoked.

Two days later, waking to the sound of the pipe, I discovered the rain had stopped! We made Grumps go to the store with us to pay for the paint for the living room ceiling and the tar. He wanted to stay home but we knew his tricks. No more " I'll pay you later." Next, we got the shingles and the green rock that Jon said was needed to repair the roof. He seemed so completely sure of himself, that I forgot one thing about him for the minute.

After a long time up on the roof he came down and was real proud of himself. He had tested it with hoses and the leak was gone!

With the help of Jon and a few chairs, I managed to get up on the flat roof to see his masterpiece. There it was! The bright green patch of rock stood out among the rest of the brown rock roof. Both Jon and Grumps are color blind, but sometimes I forget. Oh my! Being a flat roof, no one but an airplane pilot would see it, so what the heck. I congratulated him on a very good job!

Going to a McDonald's later, Jon saw the first young female in this geriatric haven, but she didn't fall head over heels for him, so I guess he was a little put out.

No rain, so Jon got the bright idea to go to Roosevelt Dam. He called Alma who was all for it. Grumps was mad because he thought people should stay home instead of running all over the place. I didn't want to go but decided that if I didn't die, I could be of help to someone when we went over the cliff. Miserable trip, but Jon and Alma loved it.

The next morning, both Jon and I were excited about going back to the frozen North. The girls would have to love Jon without a tan!

The plane had to land in Denver because of some mechanical problem. We would be there maybe four hours while they fixed the plane.

I called Bumper from Denver and told him about the delay. He said the electricity was off because of the weather and that he and Heidi were sitting wrapped up in blankets and using candles for light. I was really concerned about them catching a cold and told him to go to the Barber Shop to get warm. I guess the electricity was off all over that area. As Heidi had predicted, everything was going wrong at home!

Finally we boarded the plane and I have never had such a rotten flight and I'm not afraid of flying. Macho Jon will show no fear, so I don't know what his thoughts were when the old tub was shaking all over the sky and sounding funny. I didn't believe they had fixed it very well and was praying that it would stay up. Actually, I was petrified! Jon stayed looking calm, to calm me down.

Final approach, thank God! I had a window seat and we were almost on the ground when the plane SWOOPED up again. Now, fear was evident in everyone but Jon. He couldn't be stupid enough not to be afraid, could he? Another time around the city and we went down again and the wheels touched the ground. God was with us!!! We were alive!

We were picked up at the airport by Sonja's boyfriend Marty. He had forgotten to bring our winter coats in the freezing weather. Luckily, we had only about 50 miles to go on the icy night roads. Freezing to death was a real possibility if we were to slide off the road, but what the heck, If God wanted us, he could have had us on the plane trip home. It was a harrowing ride, but I think I had been too afraid in that plane to be afraid now.

Getting home, the electricity was back on, heat was on and Bumper, Heidi and our old black cat were all fine. Because Marty couldn't stay overnight, he headed back to the city. We were worried about his safety until he called to say he was safely home.

Home at last! Things were normal. House was a mess!

I got such a nice compliment from Heidi when I got home. She said, "I'm glad you're home. When you're gone everything goes wrong." I said, "Everything goes wrong when I'm home too." Heidi replied, "Yes, but it doesn't seem as bad when you're here. The bad things are better." I don't believe anyone could get a higher compliment than that.

BUMPERS DOG

The cute little dog that I planned would be my adorable friend, was soon Bumper's Dog, with the name COG. He wanted no one to come into the house except Bumper! When we first got him, he was sweet and gentle, but that was because he had been so abused and was happy to be anywhere that someone gave him attention. We started to notice a change in him when it would get dark. We also noticed a change in him in the day time too.

The first few days I took him to work and he was fun to have around the shop, but then, his Lhasa personality appeared and he guarded the shop and didn't want customers to come in. That didn't last long because it was bad for business. He stayed home with Bumper and cat from then on.

A few days after that, I had trouble coming home from work because he didn't want me in the house. He had either forgotten who I was, or he was guarding Bumper.

Heidi had the same problem I did, but thank God, Bumper was always home to let her in. Jon was kind of living home and kind of living with Kim and Randy in the city, Randy now going to school in Minneapolis. When Jon would come home, Cog would either bite him or pee on his leg. Poor Cog, no one liked him but Bumper and me.

In the daytime he was just sort of mean, but soon, we noticed that after dark he was a vicious little mutt. We hadn't known what a lhasa was, but we were learning fast. We found out that Lhasas' are a one-man dog and were used to guard Kings in Tibet. The King would have many of them and they could do real damage. They have an instinct to guard the King at night, lying facing the door, so no one but the King could gain power. We also learned they are called the ' Lion Dogs of Tibet.'

I hoped that maybe Cog would like me someday. Bumper let him sleep in the bed with us and he slept at his feet, head facing the door. If I moved my feet he would attack me. If I got up to go the bathroom, he wouldn't let me back in the bedroom. Bandit slept at my head and if I disturbed him, he would attack me. That is what I call a no win situation! It was a good thing I have a very good sense of humor.

One night, Ray from the ambulance came over to watch TV with us. Cog watched her every move, growling all the time. That was the last time she watched TV with us.

Bandit used to be all Bumpers and didn't pay much attention to me, but that was changing. He thought Daddy was pretty stupid for bringing in such a ridiculous live, breathing, whatever it was. He loved our big dogs, but this was certainly not a dog.

Bandit was not afraid of Cog; he just didn't like him. Bandit weighed 22 pounds and the Cog 12, so Cog was actually afraid of Bandit. Bandit always remained King of the house, with Cog just thinking he was.

I learned why Lhasa Apsos are so rare. The average life span, without a leash, is six minutes in the country, three minutes in town, because they will attack a moving car or truck. Cog even tried to attack a Sherburne County police dog on Main Street. Lucky for him I picked him up before the huge dog killed the little rat.

If he got behind a tree in the front yard he would be hopelessly lost. If a female were in heat, he would follow the scent, no matter which direction, with no thought of ever finding his way home again.

I knew we had a problem when Cog tried to mate with my stuffed Armadillo. Not only could he not tell the sex, he didn't even know the living from the dead. We had to put Half-track, the armadillo, up on a shelf, so Cog would leave it alone.

A Lhasa is never in a dog show for obedience. They don't mind. They are in a dog show for looks.

I trained Cog pretty good because if I held meat and called him, he would come if he felt like it.

Not everyone can have a dog such as this. If you are alone in a house, have no visitors, it will work. Anyone else living in, or coming to the home, must be blessed with extreme patience and humor.

We would always see ads in the newspaper to sell, or give away Lhasas, which say ' Good family pet.' We cracked up laughing and felt sorry for anyone as dumb as we were. He was so stupid, that he needed someone to love him, so we were it!

SHOP LIFE

My shop was right in the middle of Main Street. Next-door was what was called, at that time, the Buffalo House. The American Legion hall was a few doors down, on the corner of the next block. It was interesting to watch some locals go from one bar to the other. The bars always did very well in Zimmerman Minnesota.

From any church in town, the funeral procession would have to go through Main Street, so you could tell how big the funeral was. I was not nosey; I just looked out my shop window!

When men in suits walked down the street, Ray and I really took notice because that was not the normal attire for local men. We knew it was probably trouble for someone.

With me having nothing to do with it, the UPS truck used to stop very often and leave a package for someone. They said, "I'm suppose to leave it here and they'll pick it up later." I thought that was cute and I liked it!

My son Jon and some friends wanted to join a bowling league and they needed someone to sponsor them. Would I do it? Of course! They had the team for about three years and never lost their standing in the league. They even got a trophy the last year they bowled, but it was the BOOBY PRIZE, because their standing was the very bottom team the whole time. They were the worst bowlers the Princeton Lanes had ever seen. I believe they used the name Gutter Balls and it was probably the most fitting name of any team! They had beautiful shirts and looked like they were professionals! I was proud of them because most teams moved around a bit, but this one stayed right at the bottom. Consistent, dependable, I liked that!

Main Street consisted of the Buffalo House, a restaurant, which later was turned into a video store, pizza shop, hardware store, Legion Hall, Insurance office, Jednicks Construction Co., (my landlord) the newspaper office, a church and just off Main Street the Post Office, bank and laundromat, which was kind of the social club of the town.

Nonabelle and I both wrote columns for the small newspaper in town. I wrote about different people in town, so everyone would know them. Nonabelle, on the other hand, wrote the town gossip section and it was probably the most well read page. She was a cute little woman with her gray hair rolled into a bun. She would zip around town looking for all the gossip and tear down the street, her many keys dangling from a large chain around her neck. From her we would find out who ate where for dinner, who went into the city for a procto and everything else imaginable. Nonabelle would also stop in the shop and gab with us for a while. She reminded me of the little Matchmaker in Fiddler on the Roof and she would have been good at that job too.

One incident I will never forget, was when a young attractive woman came into the shop one day and asked, "Where is your other woman barber?" " I am the only full time barber here and I don't have another woman," I replied. She then said, "you must have." "No, I don't," I replied again. Then she said, " But my husband always comes home and brags about the real young, cute, barber that cuts his hair." I started laughing and said, "Lady, he is really putting one over on you." Soon, we were both laughing as hard as we could. That poor woman had heard about this woman for so long, that she finally had to have a face-to-face meeting with the beauty queen she had heard so much about. An overweight, older blond woman didn't quite fit the bill he had been talking about. She went home much happier, but I don't know if she ever let on to him that she had finally met me.

Meanwhile, Ray and I are still on the same backgammon game, but I have decided she is cheating in some way, because her luck can't be that good forever.

MOTHER IN LAWS REVENGE

My relatives are always trying to introduce me to the Arts. I have been introduced, I just don't like them! My mother-in-law was always trying to take me through the Walker Art Center, a modern art gallery, where she works as a docent taking un-suspecting people on tours. If people are going there expecting to see real true art, they are in for a big surprise. Mother-in-law was Miss Minneapolis in 1939 and still weighs the same as she did then. She was a model most of her life.

Just to make the little woman happy, I decided that for once I would do, as she wanted. Because of his health, Bumper could not walk through a gallery, but even if he had his health he wouldn't want to do it. We are very much alike. He went into the city with me and stayed at Mama's while we went to see the precious art.

Mother-in-law told us to come early and have breakfast with her. We hadn't been there for five minutes when already the beautiful, slender little woman was trying to reform me, plus make me lose weight! She had plans for me to exercise with her in the pool. Since I don't much like exercising, I was happy to tell her that I didn't bring my suit. She said she had a spare one, but no spare one of hers would even come close to fitting me, so I knew she had gone around to her larger size friends to borrow one. Since she went to all that trouble, I thought I might as well humor her.

Bumper went along to supervise, which he thinks he does very well. He sits in front of the TV telling football players how to play, coaches how to coach and announcers how to announce. When he played high school football and hockey, most of his muscles were used sitting on the bench and his face for stopping pucks and cleats.

I was thankful that the pool was empty because I didn't want anyone to see me playing with those milk bottles she brought along with her. When we were done playing with bottles, she had to teach me to do water ballet. I would have preferred a hot tub. The grueling 20 minutes of water ballet almost did me in. The things I do to keep peace with mother-in-iaw!

All that nonsense over, we had breakfast and I was famished from all that exercise. That little woman fed us grapefruit and melon. I hate grapefruit, but if I must eat it, I prefer it with sugar, but that was a no -no. Bumper loved the breakfast, so what else is new, he loves all food. Maybe by the next day I would be thin!

Mother-in- law was off that day, so she arranged a private tour for me, but I really think she didn't want me on a tour with other humans. She asked if I would like the "children's" or the "adult" tour. The adult tour would be fine, although I wasn't sure which one I had gotten on.

Entering the gallery, I stepped on a fish painted on the floor. Mother-in-law yelled and carried on about me stepping on that fish. How was I to know it was even a fish, it didn't look like any fish I have ever seen! Not only was there a fish on the floor, but also a paper -mache man, or something resembling one, hanging, or more like wafting, from the ceiling. It could have passed for a big weird looking balloon but it wasn't, because then it wouldn't have been art. The place sure didn't look like an Art Museum to me. The next room looked like a house of horrors. The paintings were just awful! There were three huge somethings on the wall, all done by the same artist, or whatever you could call him. These were all done in just two colors, black and red. The first one was painted red, with black dripping from the top. The second one was all red and could have been used for barn siding. The third was black, with a stripe of red at the top. Those atrocities sell for thousands of dollars! I used to think that the people who painted modern art were nuts, but now I have changed my way of thinking. The nuts are the people that help make them famous by telling them it's good. The true wacko's are the crazy ones that buy the stuff, for real money!

Actually, the artists are smart, because anyone could make that ugly stuff in a couple of minutes. I should paint some junk like that and get paid money for it. I know I could do just as well. Since mother-in-law loves the stuff so much, I asked her if she would actually pay the big price for this junk. She said, "Yes, if I could afford it." That should answer any questions you have about Bumper's family. I rest my case! Mother-in-law told me that the artist who painted the three awful pictures had committed suicide. I understand why. Maybe he took a good look at his painting and felt badly because he was a success at making such awful stuff, or else, he thought he was as good as Michaelangelo. If he thought that, it wouldn't be hard to understand why he wanted to meet his Maker.

The next room was a conglomeration of junkyard stuff and I mean that literally! Some crazy artist went to the junkyard, picked up trash, came home and set it in his yard for more perfection on the rust. When it was rusty enough, he welded it all together to make NOTHING!

One of mother-in-law's favorite was called 'SKY CATHEDRAL.' I couldn't see a cathedral, or even a small church in it. She thought it was mystical!

Another piece was an old rusted gate with an ax and several other tools hanging from it. If that outstanding piece of junk was sitting in my yard, I would have the trash man take it and he would charge me to do it.

The next piece was really something, from somewhere or nowhere, I don't know which. It was a mobile with three arms. One arm had a dilapidated chair hanging over it. The other an old wooden barrel, and the third arm was holding an old log.

A strange man had been making eyes at mother-in-law and I was wondering if some suspense and intrigue awaited us in this visit to the museum. Maybe I would get a good story out of this trip after all, with a stranger lurking in the shadows and following us.

Next, mother-in-law showed me two chairs; one made of yarn, the other of pins. The yarn chair was leaning toward the pin chair, which was leaning backwards. The yarn chair was attacking the pin chair, but most people would be expecting the pin to be attacking the yarn chair. What people? Who would really care? I was beginning to feel a bit edgy being with a woman that I felt was really going off the deep end and with a sinister looking man following us.

Next was a mythology sculpture called 'Mutilation.' You could tell nothing, so I supposed it was named that because the artist was in fear of being mutilated if anyone saw this mess.

Now, my private guide showed me the 'Veil Painting,' where the artist didn't use a brush, but did it on the floor with a bucket and roller. I could have told her that! Why it was called a veil, I have no idea. Probably covered up a famous painting or something good.

On the way to the next piece of culture, I had this eerie feeling of someone watching and I knew the stranger was still near. The next piece looked like diamonds inside of diamonds and was called TARGET! That was the only title that made sense, because it is exactly what I would have used if I'd had a gun or bow and arrow at my disposal. That should have been the name for all the works of art in the whole gallery!

When my guide asked me at the next one if I knew what it was, I said, "Yes, It's a bunch of dead fish surrounded by polka dots". With a look of true embarrassment mixed with horror, she said, "No, it's called 'SWIMMERS." Why it had that name, I will never guess! People that work in the gallery have to know the names and since they are told the names, they think they fit! I think they must go to a school that teaches diplomacy or something, to try to make people believe all this art is wonderful.

She thought my eyesight was failing when I couldn't see a box of cigarettes in a picture called 'CIGARETTES.' She even had me move back a ways but I still couldn't find a box, or even one cigarette.

I didn't know what Pop Art was, but when she took me to that section, I found out I hadn't missed a thing! One of those beauties was a bunch of newspaper clippings put in a frame. Original? I don't think so.

The strange man was following us, or I should say her, as we went over to the permanent art section. I knew immediately what the first sculpture was and I shouted at mother-in-law to let her know how smart I was. I yelled loud enough so everyone around us could hear. "It's the carcass of a dead roadrunner lying upside down." Mother-in-law, at that point, tried to act like she didn't know me.

The artist was very much in trouble with the next piece, because it was called, 'WOMAN.' The busts were on the backside, on the bottom of her body. The top, looked like a penguin wearing a football helmet.

The next picture did not belong in the place, because you could see a room with two people in it. How did something that sensible get into this place?

In the next section, I saw what has to be the most ridiculous piece of artwork known to man, not the ugliest, just the silliest! This artist had spent two years writing over two million numbers on paper. All the sheets of paper were stacked up on the floor, about waist high, with a paperweight on top. These papers were enclosed in a glass case as my docile docent was telling me about it. I wanted to know why he had saved all this paper? She looked at me with this

“I don’t know you” look and said, “It’s part of his collection.” It’s hard for me to visualize any sane person sitting and writing numbers for two years and even harder to believe they would keep all the paper. Maybe I should save paper, write something on it, pile it up high, put a paperweight on top and leave it at the gallery doorstep. If they thought someone famous had done it, up it would go!

I also saw a very good picture of a sailboat, but the front end was completely gone, vanished!

After what seemed like about 18 hours, the tour was finally over and as we got to the entry with the fish on the floor, the sinister looking man approached us. Maybe he was a killer coming to shoot us. He walked up to mother-in-law and said, “There is nothing prettier than a beautiful woman with wrinkles.” I would have slapped him, but mother-in-law is too polite. She was too naive to realize this man was a professional flirt. He talked and talked, while I yawned and mother-in law listened. He was jabbering on about the fact that women are best when their kids are grown. He is the kind of man I would expect to hang out in this gallery, but mother-in-law thought he was nice! I am the one that lives ‘in the sticks’? He said he was there with a date, but she must have been in his imagination only. He said they were going to a play and then a coffee house. He said she was somewhere looking at all the beautiful art. I had an imaginary friend once too, but I was much younger! I would call the old creep a pervert, but mother-in-law believed him!

From now on, I shall worry about mother-in-law every time she sets foot outside without a chaperone.

My day at the gallery was a very interesting one, to say the least! I would not put one thing from there in my house, or in my barn, if I had one. I came back with a positive attitude about modern art. I didn’t like it before, but now I was positive I didn’t like it! Next, I suppose dear mother-in-law will want to take me to a real art museum. Boy, is she in for a surprise! I won’t go if she leaves a trail of silver dollars with a rainbow and pot of gold at the end. P.T. BARNUM once said, "There's a sucker born every minute," and I made up for two whole hours that day.

Arriving back at mother-in-law's house, Bumper kept telling us to shut up, because you cannot talk during a football game. He was busy hollering at the players, telling them what they did wrong! He had gotten along very well by himself.

For mother-in-law's birthday that year, Bumper and I painted three pictures for her, which we think she loved. The only difference was, we weren't famous!

The first one was all white, painted of course. It was entitled ' White Rabbit and family, carrying cotton through a blizzard.' The second one was all black, with a sliver of moon. It was entitled, 'Black Cat Hiding behind bushes at midnight.' The third one was the most difficult. It was something that may, or may not, have been a hand reaching up to what may, or may not, have been a moon. Its title was 'Aspirations'.

They were as good, or better, than what I had seen at the Gallery. All the pictures at the gallery had titles, but you couldn't match the titles with the pictures, even if your imagination was going at full speed!

At least in our pictures, you could visualize what it was supposed to be. Actually, there ARE white rabbits and a black cat in the paintings, but only the most talented of artists would be able to detect them.

SHOP MANAGER

I decided I should make Bumper important, so I gave him the job of "Shop Manager". Important business also needs a President and a Vice President, so being the President, I installed Ray as Vice President. We were all on the Board, and I was Chairman of the Board.

Bumper was not a good manager, but I didn't have the heart to fire him, so I let him keep his title. He was supposed to record all the money into the book daily, but he didn't. Only once in a while! He was also supposed to get things ready to take to the taxman. He had orders from the boss not to order everything anyone tried to sell over the phone. He was worthless! Every time one of those bimbo's would call and offer a chance on a big prize if you bought their products, he would order plenty of it. We ended up with more and more stuff that the only thing we could do with it was give it away. We even had bubble gum for the kids.

One day, I came in when Bumper was making one of his big orders. I was hoping my hard of hearing ears were deceiving me when he was talking. When he hung up, he was all excited about a deal from some super salesman. He had ordered pens, with the shop name on, for $200.00. You had a chance for a big prize if your name was picked. "How many pens do you get for that money"? I asked. He didn't know, but the prizes were good. First Prize was a trip for two to the Greek Isles. I would have loved to go there, but would need to take a second job to get the necessary spending money and Bumper wasn't well enough to go. I don't think anyone would ever win it! Next prize, a 25-inch T.V., that no one would win either and we didn't need it. The next prize was a sauna for two. Wonderful, our house would be too small for one and both Bumper and I hated saunas. No one probably won it anyway. Next prize, a ten minute shopping spree in a grocery store. “Where is the grocery store”? I asked. He didn’t know, so it probably was in East Overshoe, Alaska, if there was such a place! No one probably won! Last prize, and cheap, I was sure, was a nine-piece Black and Decker tool set. Wonderful! Whatever tools were in there, Bumper would never use, even if he knew how. Then came a cash prize of $700.00 that I was sure they would want you to use to buy more stuff. I made Bumper call up slick Dick in California and cancel the order. He didn’t like it, but he had to do it. Ray was in the shop through this whole melee, and I thought she would choke from laughing and that I would have to revive her.

When he got the super salesman of the year on the phone, he said, “My wife says I don’t know anything about tools, I won’t fit in the sauna, I’m afraid to fly, I don’t need a T.V. and as far as a grocery spree in concerned, if I could get there, I would get everything I’m not allowed to have and my doctor would kill me, the dog house would be too crowded for me to live in and so I have to cancel the order.” After that, he was better.

Ray complained all the time that she should get wages as vice president, but like Bumper, she didn’t do anything. I told her she would get a raise one of these days, but she said, “100% of nothing, is still nothing.” Good help was sure hard to get in those days. With the capable help I had, I was glad my shop was small, so I could do everything myself.

I knew Ray had to be cheating and I demanded that we start a new backgammon game after all that time. She wouldn’t agree, I would have to put more pressure on her.

JON

At six feet two, Jon is the typical blond haired, well built, strong Norwegian/American, with a good disposition.

Jon had finished mechanics school and was now working. We thought he should move to Minneapolis so he would be closer to his work, but he hadn't decided to leave home yet. He claimed he wanted his own apartment, but didn't really look for one. Would he ever leave the nest, I thought?

When he wanted to borrow Bumper's cowboy boots and we said "no", we thought he would get mad and run away, but Jon said, "If you give me the boots to keep, I'll move." It was tempting, but Bumper loved those boots as much as he loved eating.

Jon stayed in the city one night with Sonja and Randy and the windows on his truck, except for one front and one side window, were shot out. Three cars were hit that same night. Thank God the vehicles were all without people in them. What if someone had been in the cars or just out walking, or a bullet had gone through someone's house window? Again, we have to thank God!

Since the truck was old and the insurance expensive, Jon had liability coverage only. Replacing the windows would be costly and he needed to save money for the apartment he would someday have. His choice was to be warm while driving or to live on his own. Maybe he would be home forever. Driving to work with plastic on the windows was really cold in the Minnesota winter. The plastic wouldn't stay on, so the cold brisk air hit him. His throat was sore all winter, but he knew it would go away by spring. In the spring, he planned to park the truck and drive his precious Trans Am, which is not a good car for winter. That Trans Am was his pride and joy and we knew he would want to park it in the yard for the rest of his life.

The next night, Harvey called and asked Jon if he would go to French Morocco with him. Jon never shows excitement, but we could tell he was elated. He said, "Where is French Morocco"? I knew where Morocco was, so some part of it must be French. They would "sight-see" in Morocco and from Casablanca, go to Spain where Harvey would leave Jon to "sight-see". Harvey would go to Israel to join my sister Lori, who was already there visiting my niece Kyra and her husband, who live in Israel.

Harvey had taken all the kids to distant lands when they were in High School. They went on an African Safari and went trekking through the Himalayas. Sonja, because of her heart, didn't go on those trips, but they took her to Mexico, which was closer to American doctors.

Since Jon had been to Israel, my little tyke would see Spain all by himself. He accidentally had this huge hotel suite that was supposed to be for Lori and Harvey, before the plans had changed, so he lived in luxury.

As a mother I had something to worry about, because Jon couldn't speak Arabic and they probably couldn't speak much English there. I would have to wait until the little macho man got home to see if he survived.

Planning and getting him ready for the trip was pure joy, even though I was not the one going. Harvey and Lori travel all over the world and my kids have sure gotten an education because of them.

Maybe someday, I will travel to some foreign land. That was my dream!

Having our house with just Heidi, dog and cat in it, was nice for that short time.

Living his trip with him on his return was wonderful. How I would love to have money and a healthy Bumper, so we could travel.

GRANDPA'S RETURN

Embarrassment, humiliation, wanting to climb into a hole and hide my head, infuriation, laughter, needless fear and pity, these were all my feelings within the first few minutes after Grandpa got off the plane from his flight from Arizona.

It was sad to see how such a well-groomed, loving man could go so far downhill after Mother's death. He was not always like this. Two flight attendants brought him to me, holding on to his arms. I was afraid that maybe he was sick or had had a stroke. He looked as if he had thrown up all over himself, but with a closer look I saw it was just dirt, and meals from the last couple of days. Not having his own personal, free barber in Arizona, "me", his hair was in dire need of a cut. It looked like it was purposely groomed to stand up on the top of his head. Except for the color, his hair resembled Don King's! He hadn't shaved since his cleaning lady packed for him two days before, nor had he changed his clothes. Grumps can make a mess of his clothes after eating one meal, or after changing his pipe tobacco, so a couple of days in this same attire and he looked like a reject from the bum colony under the bridge.

When the flight attendants came with him, they told me, "He is very disoriented, so you should watch him." As I sat him in the nearest chair, I was calculating where the closest hospital was and the quickest way to get to it. An elderly woman motioned to me to come over and she said she had sat with Grumps during the flight. "Are you the sister that was picking him up?' she asked me. " No, but I'm his daughter. There is no sister involved." She also said, "He was fine until his third bottle of airline whiskey." MY DAD DOESN'T DRINK!

You get two drinks out of each bottle of airline whiskey, so that meant he had consumed six drinks. Grumps was so cheap, I couldn't see him paying for it. I would never have guessed that he was totally pickled! I asked him if he had had a drink on the plane. I was now close enough to smell his breath when he answered, "No, I slept the whole time." I almost fell over from the smell of whiskey. I decided to just let him think he was pulling the wool over my eyes. He could never win an Oscar for his acting performance of trying to appear sober. What would the doctors in the emergency room have thought if I had brought the old curmudgeon in, thinking he was sick?

While waiting for the skycap to come with a riding cart, I heard an awful pounding sound, reverberating through the whole gate area. When I turned around, there was Grumps pounding the ashes out of his pipe into a metal trashcan. He managed to catch the attention of everyone else in the entire area too.

When the cart arrived, I put Grumps into it, holding on to him so he wouldn't fall out. I was carrying the carry-on bag that my sister Lori had given him for Christmas that he hated. It was too expensive and ruined his image as a street beggar. He was carrying a brown paper sack, which I was curious about. I hoped that he could hang on to it.

In Phoenix, he didn't have to tip the skycaps, because in his ragged condition while standing and turning his pockets inside out, they felt sorry for him. He sure wouldn't tip with me there, so I reached into my purse. As I was doing that, he started to get up, and dropped his brown paper bag. It really made a mess! Cookies, potato chips, candy and a sandwich went rolling all over the floor. I hurriedly paid the skycap so we could get out of there. Why did he have his cleaning lady pack a lunch for his three-hour trip, when a meal would be served in flight? With all the drinking he had done, I didn't think he had time to eat the food that Northwest Airlines had provided. Maybe he had just slept?

I suppose people wondered what kind of children this old man had, who would allow him to run around in dirty ragged clothes? They probably thought he also lived in a dump with no water, so he couldn't clean himself.

I carefully propped Grumps into a chair at the Baggage Claim and went to retrieve his precious bags. I knew what they looked like. When we came to Phoenix with Grumps, the Airline had lost his bags and delivered them to the house the next day. I was truly embarrassed describing them. They looked even worse after his return flight. The hinges on the old white Samsonite were broken. Clothes were hanging out from all sides and it was tied together with a dilapidated belt. I couldn't imagine the ticket agent allowing it to be checked. His other bag, a garment bag, was rolled up in a ball and tied with a ratty looking brown belt. Both bags had bright orange ribbons on them for identification, which really weren't needed. No one in their right mind would steal those bags, unless they would think the Smithsonian would take them. He resembled a character out of 'THE GRAPES OF WRATH.'

I picked them off the carousel as fast as I could, hoping no one would see me. I trusted that Grumps would stay in the same spot where I had left him, which usually was not a problem, because other than smoking, his hobby was sitting. In his drunken condition, I didn't know what to expect, but thankfully he was still there.

My only remaining problem was how to get Grumps and his luggage to the car, because I didn't dare leave him sitting alone while I drove the car around to pick him up. I had to take everything at once! I was dressed in the beautiful clothes that my sister Lori had sent to me. I managed to hold on to my big purse, his two ridiculous suitcases and Grumps. Not only was it hard, I know I must have looked pretty silly wandering around looking for my car with all that luggage and Grumps. It's a good thing I was dressed nicely, or people might have thought I was heading for a beat up, old rusted pick-up truck.

It would have even been funnier if Lori had been the one picking up this ragged man. What would she have done? I honestly don't know, but since she's a millionaire, I think she would have paid someone a nice sum to retrieve the bags, drive around and have that person slip them quickly into the trunk of her Caddie. Maybe, she would have just skipped the baggage claim, left his bags there and bought him new clothes, which would really have made him mad. He doesn't like new clothes; he likes the old ones that protect his image.

I did know that if Mother was looking down from heaven, there would be a big fight inside the Pearly Gates when her husband showed up. She would not approve of the way he had been acting since she had died, and would certainly let him have it. I hope someone will be able to stop the chaos that could happen up there.

Grumps was tired. He had gotten up at 4:00 A.M., to make sure he wouldn't miss his noon flight. He had nothing to get ready! His cleaning woman picked him up at 9:00 A.M. to take him on the short trip to the airport. He liked to get there plenty early so he won't worry about missing the plane. He had called me every night for the last week to make sure I would be at the airport. Why he did that, I don't know, because I was always there to take him anywhere he had to go. I suppose when he got to the airport, he sat and worried about whether or not I would be waiting for him.

I was glad that he was safely home, in the senior citizen apartment where he lived. It was nice to have him gone for a few months though, because I picked him up every Sunday and holidays to be with us, and having a rest was nice.

Two days after he was home, he called to let me know that he was just tired when he landed, in case he acted a little funny. He still wouldn't own up to having had even one drink!

We are very fortunate, because most families have one nut in the family, but we have several!

SONJA'S SURGERY

The day that we hoped would make Sonja healthy finally came.

She was engaged to a boy that everyone loved. Marty and I would be at the University hospital during the operation and the rest of the kids would have a normal day, but they would be where we could keep in touch with them. Bumper would get too nervous sitting in the surgery waiting room, so Heidi stayed home with him to try to keep him calm. I don't think he ever left the chair by the phone at all that day.

It was a tense, terror filled, yet exciting wait. Would she finally be healthy? Would she survive the surgery? What if we hadn't gotten her to Dr.Azzam? Although I was used to hospital waiting rooms by this time, it was not easy. The only consolation was that there was no other option. She was frightened of surgery, but was afraid not to have it, knowing her life would be considerably shortened without it. In front of us she was brave and strong.

The surgery took about five of the longest hours I have ever spent in my life. During the long wait I kept in touch with everyone, but could only tell them that they had to wait longer. At least they knew things were going well.

After what seemed to me like ten years, her surgeon, Dr. Molina from the University, came out and told us that the surgery had gone well and that she should recover nicely. We couldn't ask any questions and he was almost to the point of being rude, but he was just going in to do another surgery immediately. He had just saved my daughter's life; I didn't care about how rude he had seemed, or his impatience. I loved that man completely. It's easy to understand why he was too busy to talk to us.

Doctor Molina and his team had rerouted her heart so it would work well with only three chambers. It was now working exactly like a snake's heart, because a snake has three chambers to the heart. Crying was very acceptable at that emotional moment.

Previously, I had seen Bumper hooked up to heart & lung machines and that was a horror for me. Seeing your own child hooked up to all of that equipment is even worse. I, her mother, could do nothing to help or comfort her.

The next day she was taken off most of the life support equipment. She looked much better and even knew what was happening around her. She was so weak that I thought she would be in the hospital for a long time, but I was wrong. A total of five days and the doctor said she could leave the hospital if she came to our house where I could care for her.

On her third day in the Hospital, our son Jon had gone to visit her. When he took her for a ride in the wheel chair, she found out that her heart worked very well. Macho boy had decided to run down the halls and do wheelies with her in the wheel chair. She has never forgotten and never will forget that ride. She was quite scared, because she knew her brother and knew he was a daredevil. The hospital staff were running around trying to stop the little fool. Everyone that day thought her heart had been fixed quite well. I am thankful I was not there at the time to witness that great event.

When the five days were up, I was terrified to take her home because I thought she was released too soon. That wonderful Doctor Wang knew what he was doing. She stayed in bed a couple of days at home, then got up and started doing her normal routine things she had always done. She found she had more strength than she had ever had in her entire life. Sonja had never felt this good and became anxious to get back to her own apartment. She also was going to be making plans for her wedding, which was to take place in about six months. My daughter was healthy and stronger than I had ever known her to be.

Sonja is truly a medical wonder because very few people have been born with only three chambers to their heart. Most who were, died shortly after birth, and it was rare to survive to adulthood. A very small number of surgeries similar to Sonja's had been done throughout the world, but Sonja's was one of the most successful.

Dr. Wang was pleasantly surprised to see her on a ski slope six months later. Before the surgery, she had been unable to do that.

How blessed my family is! God has always been there for us when we needed Him.

Can Bumper ever be this well, I wondered? How fortunate I am. Now, I thought, I only have one person's health problem to worry about.

WHITE DOG AND WHITE DOG LADY

When the kids were small, Bumper got a CB base radio. We were often "snowed in" during the winter and it was a good thing to have for highway emergencies and other urgent needs. When the kids were older, putting CB's in their cars helped to avoid stress for Bumper. When they were off somewhere, or on the way home from work at night, they would let Bumper know where they were. CB's were good, because living off the main road we could get help immediately if any of the family were to go into the ditch on icy roads.

We also had fun with our CB. Especially me!

Very early in the morning, before I'd leave for the Barber Shop, I would get on the CB. I would sing. The truckers always said that I almost put them into the ditch, but they wanted more. I would sing one rendition of Indian Love Call that was the worst one ever heard. Then I would start talking because everyone kept asking me questions. It really became an early morning show. The callers wanted my description. They didn't know whether to believe it or not, but it was accurate. I said, "Slightly heavy, beautiful, around the house I wear an old nightie and un-matched socks. I do not wear my teeth when talking on the CB, but my beauty soars when I have them in." Local people were even tuning in and I heard about myself in the Barber Shop. Customers and the ambulance crew would talk about this nutty woman who was on the CB in the morning, but no one knew who she was, only that she lived near Zimmerman, my home town.

Joy, a member of the Ambulance crew wanted to find out who the nutty woman was. I enjoyed the whole thing, because everyone was in love with White Dog Lady. Bumper was White Dog, but he wasn't usually up at that time, so he didn't hear what was going on.

In an attempt to drive Joy nuts, I put signs on her car, "White dog Lady was here." I did that a lot. Then, since I knew Joy's address, I would go to her house when no one was home and put a sign on the door, "White Dog Lady was here". She didn't suspect me, because I sounded so different without teeth! Bumper soon got in on it too, and started talking on the morning show, and he can disguise his voice very well. For a few months, we were driving many people in town crazy. Finally, We showed up at Joy's door and announced who we were. She could have killed us, because she had been talking to me about White Dog Lady for several months.

The ambulance crew did get even with us though. One morning while I was gabbing on the CB, they quickly drove up the driveway, raced to the door and Bumper let them in. They had to see if I really dressed as badly as I said I did, and they soon discovered that I hadn't lied. There I was, a house full of company, old ragged flannel gown, un-matched socks full of holes, no teeth, uncombed hair and a messy house. What a way to start a morning before going to work, but I had that one coming. We all had a good laugh.

I had known Joy for some time, but because of all that, we became fast friends. We would go to their house and they would come to ours for dinner, cards or whatever.

My anonymous days as White Dog Lady were over, but it had been fun being a celebrity, although unknown, for a while. Being famous agrees with me.

One day Joy stopped in when I was in the process of wallpapering the kitchen. I had picked out paper with a beautiful pattern of blue birds flying all over it. Bumper was watching me and giving his advice, but, since he would never do any of the work, I had no intention of listening to him. To me, the idea of putting up wallpaper was to make the wall nice and clean and fresh. I was doing that.

In came Joy and started screaming, saying that I couldn't do that. I asked, "What can't I do?" She said. "Look at it, all the birds are flying upside down and backwards and you don't have the pattern matched." I had only done one small wall, but my kitchen, as well as all the other rooms, was tiny. She babbled on, saying that I could not do that. I hate painting, wallpapering and most things considered work, so I thought it looked fine. I told her, "People shouldn't come over to bad mouth my birds. Who cares if they fly upside down, they are free flying birds."

That wonderful woman actually told us to get out of the house, as she would do it, but she didn't want us telling her what to do.

Bumper and I did just that. We went to town and hung around, while Joy did the wallpapering. When we got home, the kitchen wall had birds of a feather all going the right way and the trees matched, instead of leaves on one tree on the trunk of another. She even hung the curtains. That is a true friend, but which of us was the smarter one?

HEIDI

Jon again moved to the city, this time permanently, perhaps, but we wouldn't hold our breath. Heidi was now Queen of the Castle. She had always been happy with the tiny room she had shared with Sonja, but one day, she told us she was moving into the spare room because her room was too cold. That was surprising to us, but it would be OK if she switched rooms. If Jon returned, she would have to move back into hers.

After a few days, I decided to see just how cold her room was, so I made the mistake of opening the door. My God! It was a nightmare! Her clothes were all over everything! The bunk bed was not to be seen, nor was the carpet. The dressers were nowhere in sight, either. Poor Bandit, the cat, couldn't even jump up on anything because there was no room. Bumper and I got so mad; we piled her clothes on the living room floor and told her to put all of them away. After that was done, she had to clean her room. After it was cleaned up, she decided to move back into it because it looked so nice.

Heidi was now a senior in High School, working at a Pizza shop late at night on weekends. She then decided she wanted to go to college, because staying with Sonja at Hamline University in St. Paul had been fun, so she thought that college might be a blast. Her grades were very poor because she had never cared much about school and definitely was not a scholar! The only college that would accept her was River Falls at Wisconsin. We were all in a state of shock, because we just didn't know how she would ever pass any course in college. Time would tell!

Heidi had long flowing blonde hair, was tall and very pretty.

Sonja and Heidi looked a lot alike, so it was no wonder that boys were always around them. She had some boyfriends, but we always wondered about her taste in males.

One came to pick her up and Bumper started talking to him about his experience in Viet Nam. Now Bumper was definitely too old to have been in Viet Nam, unless he had been some big officer or something. He told this boyfriend that he had fought in Viet Nam and killed a whole lot of people with his bare hands. He continued talking about how dangerous and tough he was. He also said that at one time, they had gotten so hungry that they ate the people they had killed. No one, in any sane state of mind, would believe the stories he told. He made it sound like he was better than Rambo! This poor kid was buying the whole story, hook, line and sinker, and kept asking Bumper stupid questions. I often worried about Heidi! She had to agree he was not the pick of the litter.

She was happy that Bumper hadn't sat on the porch with a shotgun, like he had done one night when Sonja had a date. When the guy walked right up to the porch. Bumper knew he had guts.

Heidi's next boyfriend was one that Sonja had rejected. I guess he just wanted to stay in the family. He was a wealthy businessman, who adored both the girls, but Heidi finally gave him the brush after he said he wanted to buy her a new car when she got to college. The next one was a short little Spanish guy, living with his mother and raising his three children. Maybe his profession was as a shepherd or something, because that's what he looked like. We were greatly concerned that time! Was Heidi sane, or was she playing with a deck of only 49 cards?

We were worried that she would flunk out the first semester, but she liked it so much that she actually studied. When she wanted to go back the second year, we were flabbergasted!

Uncle Harvey had given each of our kids a car. He had kept Heidi's car in his name, which meant he was receiving all of her parking tickets. He mentioned once that there were many tickets, and we thought he was kidding. Finally, we found out that she had gotten so many tickets, that his patience had run out, and that she would have to put the car in her name and pay for the insurance. I think she had been parking any-place where the car would fit, anywhere at all. Soon, the tickets were coming to our house, because that was her home address, although she lived at the college. It was good thing too, because she would have been in jail if we hadn't gotten after her to pay them. She paid every single one. It didn't take the police long to recognize her car. She was well known in their ranks. When she finished her two years, I called the Police Chief, and told him that the city would be losing money with her gone. I suggested they build a parking ramp with all the money from her tickets.

She did find a boyfriend at school in River Falls, but we hadn't met him yet. She continued on in school at McConnell Airline School so she could become a travel agent.

THE TURKEY CATCH

In 1980, our Thanksgiving turkey was a very special one, caught with my own bare hands!

One beautiful, very warm, early fall afternoon, Bumper and I were on our way to the nearby town of Princeton. A truck, full of turkeys in wooden cages, piled on top of each other, with feathers flying all around, was ahead of us. All of a sudden a turkey fell out of the truck. The cage was smashed into kindling and the turkey ran out into the ditch. None of his friends joined him. I yelled to Bumper to stop the car, since the driver didn't miss the turkey, it would be a nice Thanksgiving treat.

I had on high heels, a skirt, a sweater and looked especially nice in a chubby way. I knew nothing about turkeys, but knew that I wanted to get hold of that bird. He was running around like crazy and flapping those huge wings. He was really giving me a run for my money.

I noticed, as busy as I was chasing that turkey, that many cars had stopped. They may have wanted my turkey, but I wasn't going to give him up. Bumper said that when the cars stopped, he should have charged admission to watch this escapade, but the road was public.

I almost had the turkey once. I had both wings in my hands for a minute but then he raised them up which scared the crap out of me. That was not going to stop me. He was the biggest bird I had ever laid eyes on. I knew that I was bigger than he was, so I got into the turkey race again.

More cars kept stopping. I suppose I looked rather stupid chasing a large turkey around that field. I would close in on him and then he would flap those big huge wings again and head the other way. We were to do the same charade again and again and each time the turkey would elude me.

By now, I thought that Bumper didn't want anyone to know that the crazy woman running around in high heels and a skirt, chasing a big bird, was his beautiful bride.

I fell onto the ground as I was grabbing him, and closed my arms around those big wings of his. I have to admit that I was scared, because I didn't know whether or not turkeys could bite. I forgot for a few minutes that they had claws. Old Tom was turning his neck in all directions, kicking and scratching me, pecking at my face, but I was not going to be a chicken now. No way! I had my catch, and he was not going to get away. I felt like the worlds biggest game hunter.
As I was quite a distance from the car I had to fight with Tom every step of the way back to the road. Do you think anyone would come to help me? No! They were probably jealous, because the bird was mine now! Bumper was such a big help. He opened the trunk door after I screamed at him to do so! He even shut it! Without him, I would never have been able to catch that turkey!

I was clean and well groomed when I entered the one-woman turkey race, but I looked a little different at the end of the battle. I was a mess! My hair was all over the place and I had hay or something from the field all over my clothes. My nylons were torn, but the pride in my face must have been evident. Not everyone catches his or her own Thanksgiving Day feast.

Getting to Princeton, we had some things to do, so we hoped that Big Tom would be quiet, stop all the kicking and carrying on, because we didn't want some officer of the law to wonder if we had kidnapped someone. Tommy decided to take a nap, so he was fine.

Figuring out what to do with the large bird when we got home was a mystery to both of us. We knew an older kid from the neighborhood, so we phoned him and asked him to come over. He opened the trunk, grabbed the irate kicking, wing flapping, big bird. Then, he very swiftly wrung his neck, so that Tommy felt nothing. That was a comfort to me, because I didn't want him to suffer. It went so fast that Tom hadn't felt a thing!

Tom stayed in the freezer for a couple of months and when Thanksgiving approached, I thawed him out. He was full of pinfeathers, which I knew nothing about, and didn't think anyone else did either. Bumper and I spent most of the night before Thanksgiving trying to pull the pinfeathers out with tweezers. That didn't work well and we knew we could never get all of them out by morning, so we pulled off all the skin from Tom.

I put big skinless Tom into the oven very early the morning of Thanksgiving. We had weighed him on the bathroom scale before cooking him and he weighed 20 pounds. I knew he was big, but I wonder how much he had weighed when I caught him.

The kids picked up Grumps (their grandfather) and came home for a good Thanksgiving dinner. They laughed when they saw the skinless bird, but he tasted wonderful. The kids and Grumps all got a chuckle over how hard Mother had worked to get this dinner for them.

Later, we found out that hot wax would have eliminated all the pinfeathers, but we wouldn't have known how to do that either.

Thank you Tom, it was nice of you to be here for dinner!

WINE, WOMEN & SONG

My first husband had many problems, the biggest one being that he was not a good husband. Maybe I had expected better of him than working as a cab driver after four years of college. Of course, with that taxi job, he was able to live the lifestyle he wanted: Wine, women and partying, although the beverage was beer, not wine, unless no beer was available.

I think he finally had figured out the marriage was over when I packed up all his clothes, cracked eggs over them, poured ketchup on them, also added a couple cans of spaghettios to the mess for good measure. I called a cab, and had them delivered to his girlfriend. I think he got the picture that you can't have a wife, a mistress and several girlfriends and stay married. This girlfriend became wife # 2 and had been a friend of mine. Our friendship ended in a hurry when the double life they were leading came to my attention. This woman had some kids that her ex-husband raised, but she saw them once in a while. Our divorce took place, but he was a no-show. There was nothing to divide, because he didn't have anything. Whoopee! I got 100% of nothing!

Bumper knew my ex through some people he knew but didn't think much of him, because he talked about his wife and his girlfriend. After I dumped him, Bumper found out where I lived and stopped over to see if I was as bad as ex had made me out to be. Bumper fell in love with my kids first. He adored them. He felt sorry for me, but soon that all changed, and he loved me as much as he loved the kids. He even fell in love with our big white dog, Sam. The kids loved Bumper, too.

I married Bumper when Heidi was two years old, Jon was six,

Sonja eight and Randy was nine. He adored me and all of our lives changed for the better when Bumper came along. He was the best thing that could have happened to me. I did, always have, and always will, love him.

After we had been married about two years, my ex married his mistress, so she became # 2. She actually did me a favor, because if that hadn't happened, I wouldn't have met Bumper.

RANDY

Randy is quiet and kind of shy, light brown hair, a good student and has a docile personality. He is one that during a tornado warning, when they say 'Take Cover', would rather stand outside and watch what is going on. I always thought he would take up meteorology instead of computers. He didn't, although he still likes to watch the weather. Most people don't love storms, but he does. He didn't have to study to get good grades, but staying outside during terrible weather, must say something about his common sense.

When he was a senior in high school, my brother-in-law, Harvey, took Randy to Thailand. He had a wonderful trip, learned a lot and got bit by a monkey.

We didn't think anything about the bite, because he was fine until two weeks later. He woke up one morning and his arm was swollen to the size of a football. I took him to Princeton Hospital Emergency room. They admitted him to the hospital and put him in isolation. We told the Doctor that it could be from a monkey bite, but he didn't want to take samples and send to the U. " It probably is that, but, I don't care what it's from, we have to give him huge doses of antibiotic to get rid of it." He was very sick and full of infection. My fear grew by the minute. It was scary for a few days, but they did get the infection under control. What a relief! After a one-week stay in the Hospital, he was glad to be home and wanted to eat, because the food they served in the Hospital was not what he would have preferred to eat. Making a "take out" restaurant with any hospital food would not be a good idea. I didn't know until then that

I was such a good cook, because he even liked my "homemade" canned soup! Well, it was cooked on my stove!

Randy, like Jon, didn't have a girlfriend in high school. I wasn't worried about him getting one, but wasn't real happy when his choice became his step sister, whom he had met at his dad's house. She was the daughter of wife # 2. Very pretty, but I was afraid she may have her mother's temperament.

My kids were all close and spent a lot of time with each other, so they knew before too long, that this was not a good match. We all tried to convince him that there were other choices, but he thought that he was in love so our advice was to no avail. They continued to go together.

Randy and Jon both went with Harvey to India, then went trekking with him through the Himalayas in Nepal. Though my boys usually don't show much emotion, the trips they went on with their uncle, really excited them.

Randy, like Jon, is color blind, but not to the degree that Jon is. During high school, one neighbor by the lake asked the boys if they wanted a job painting the porch while they were on vacation. They agreed on the job and the price, so the boys were busy painting the back patio. Bumper and I forgot about the color blindness, so we didn't think of it, until they were done and proud of their job. They wanted to show us their handwork.

We took a look at the job they were so proud of and didn't say a word for a few minutes. We just kind of nodded our heads and smiled.

Later, when the boys were gone for the day, we picked up some paint and headed for the house on the lake. The railings were supposed to be green and the rest brown. As long as the paint cans weren't full of paint and they could read the color, they were fine, but when the cans got spilled on, then watch out! They had green where it should have been brown, brown where it should have been green and green and brown where it should have been one or the other. We didn't want to hurt their feelings, because they had worked so hard on this project and they couldn't help that they are colorblind. We re-painted the porch and not one person has known about it, until now.

Bumper had a collection of Playboy magazines, and one day, he discovered that all the centerfolds were missing. Jon never showed much interest in those magazines, but Randy liked them. We never found out who the culprit was, until we heard about boys buying Playboy Centerfolds for two dollars at school.

Whichever son was the enterprising young man was pretty smart. The magazine in those days cost $1.75 and he sold the centerfolds for $2.00.

SONJA'S WEDDING

The Big day finally arrived! Harvey & Lori flew in from Chicago, along with my nieces, Subie, and their other daughter from Israel, Kyra, her husband MoMo, and two year old Mayaan.

Also coming from Chicago was Marty's family. Marty's Rabbi who would perform the ceremony along with Pastor Tom, would fly in later.

The Wedding was held in Como Park Conservatory, which is right next to the zoo, so you could say, she was married at the zoo! The Conservatory is a beautiful indoor garden, with a waterfalls and stream. Sonja was elegant in her gown, but she had been nervous about her scar going up to her neck, from the heart surgery. I told her she should be proud of that scar. Stand tall and let it be seen. That scar was the reason she was alive! She listened to her mother and the scar was insignificant.

The kids had paid for most of the wedding themselves. Everyone was very nervous, because the Rabbi didn't arrive until just before the wedding. There was no rehearsal and no one knew how they were going to do this very different ceremony. Pastor Tom and the Rabbi talked a couple minutes before the event, so they figured it out, but no one else knew.

Things were going beautifully, until some of the free flying birds in the place decided to relieve themselves. It was hard not to laugh, in fact, everyone did laugh when a bird crapped on the head of a bald guy in the wedding party. He took a hankie out of his pocket, as though nothing had happened, and wiped his head. The next shot hit a neighbor woman of ours who had just had her hair done, but she was in the rear area, so not everyone saw that. Bumper didn't miss it though, because although there was no seating in the conservatory, they did get a chair for him in the back. (In case he didn't feel well, and had to get out of the crowd.) The third shot hit another woman, also in the back of the room. I didn't blame them if they were angry, but no one complained.

The Pastor and the Rabbi married them. They ended the service with each one saying the benediction, one in Hebrew, the other one in English.

They planned to have a reception line outside the door, but all the bridesmaids disappeared, leaving only Sonja and Marty in line.

The reception was on a boat at Lake Minnetonka. We had figured that everything would be on the boat and ready when we got there, but not knowing how long the wedding would take, everyone arrived too early. We had to hang out for almost an hour before we could get on the boat.

Ray and a bunch of the ambulance crew were there to get the tables set up. They were guests as far as eating, drinking and everything else. I had asked for more crew than Ray to come, just in case Bumper needed help during that time. He didn't pick up on that reason and just thought they were there to get things set up. I had secretly arranged with the captain to stay close to the dock on the three-hour cruise. No one but the captain and I knew that we were going in large circles, instead of the usual cruise on the lake. It was night; champagne was flowing, so not one person knew the difference.

A few of us had great concerns about this boat trip, because my sister and Harvey didn't care for my ex-husband and his wife. I had little to do with my ex-husband and nothing to do with wife # 2. Lori had no time for Marty's father, knowing him from Chicago. Grandpa was certainly not enamored with my ex husband, Some of us weren't happy about Randy's choice for a girlfriend, which was the daughter of my ex's second wife, which made her his step sister. We figured their real dad, husband of #2, would get drunk, but hoping he wouldn't make a complete idiot of himself. My ex in-laws were there, Mother-in-Law was there with Bumper's sister Leslee. I didn't want my ex to look too spacey. I guess I was afraid someone would push some one off the boat and it was up in the air who? Ray knew all the tension going on, so the heck with the regular champagne glasses. She thought big water glasses would work better, so she started them out and things did start to improve. Everyone seemed to be getting along. Ex got loaded but he was just the normal friendly drunk that he is.

Bumper stayed on the open upper deck which gave him plenty of fresh air, and worked well to separate people that didn't like each other.

I felt much safer having the ambulance crew there and they also kept the place hopping.

Reception was over and no one drowned, or was pushed off the boat. The kids were married and nothing left but the mess. A ton of food and champagne, beer and drinks were left over, so the ambulance crew took all of it back and had it for all the crews to enjoy the next day.

Heidi had fallen in love with a friend of Marty's from Chicago. I didn't think she'd ever find a guy she would keep. She liked to play the field and her choices hadn't been too good.

Jon never had a girlfriend, and I thought he was to shy to get one. If the two of them ever get married, I'm sure it would be a double wedding at some McDonalds.

It was wonderful seeing Kyra, Subie, Lori and Harvey, but then we had to part. It was also great seeing MoMo and two year old Maayan, except I hated a kid that could understand two languages,

Hebrew and English. It made me jealous!

The End of a Beautiful Affair!

THE MOUSE

Hermits, who have been hibernating all winter, come out in the spring for a haircut, because they reach a point where it cannot be combed.

My yearly cabin dweller showed up at the barber shop again, with his hair down to the middle of his back. Getting a comb or brush through it was impossible so I checked for lice and found none. The only thing I could do was, to hold up one chunk of hair at a time, and just cut it off, before I was able to wash it.
He must have sat in his cabin all winter, because his clothes reeked of the smoke from the wood he used in his potbelly stove. It was June now, and his clothes still smelled of wood smoke.

His hair needed three washings in order to get it clean, and after a year it must have felt good to have a comb go through his hair. Last year, it hadn't been cut very short, and that is why this ungodly mess was before me. After washing it and cutting off the first clump, I cut it short. Except for the smell and the dirty clothes, he almost looked respectable. He was nice enough, just kind of eccentric.

After he left, I was sweeping up the hair, and while picking it up to put in the bin, spotted something that I was sure I hadn't seen. I couldn't have seen it! I was not dreaming, so I took a closer look to see what I thought I had seen. I'm not telling a lie at all when I say I found a dead mouse in that long messy hair. It had been there a long time and was rather dried up. Maybe that is one reason he smelled so bad, but then, I think it was too old to smell anymore. The mouse must have become strangled in that long, dirty, messy, mangy, hanging mass of hair. I cannot believe he couldn't feel a mouse trying to get out. It must have taken a long time for it to die in there.

Can you imagine what it would smell like after it had been dead for a few days?

This happened to be one of the few times neither Ray nor Bumper were in the shop. I called Ray downstairs in the ambulance barn, and told her to get up to the shop. I knew I would be called a liar if I didn't have a witness to this unholy scene. I just showed her my catch of the day, without telling whose head it had come from. "Oh my God! What should we do, stuff it or freeze it?" she said.

I was glad I hadn't discovered little Minnie when the guy was in the shop, because I didn't know how I would tell someone that they had a dried up old mouse in their hair. I don't know if I would have said something or not. It would have been embarrassing for both of us, I am sure.

I am thankful that I had time to sterilize everything and get the shop cleaned up before another customer came in.

I called Bumper and told him about Minnie, and he thought I must have gone off the deep end, but Ray had been there for proof.

EUROPE

Harvey offered Bumper and me a trip to Hawaii a few weeks after Sonja's wedding. We were thrilled. Traveling to any destination was something I would have loved to do. With Bumper's bad heart, it was out of the question, and saying "No" to that wonderful offer was hard for me to do.

Maggie, my friend from Princeton told me about an Oblate Mission trip to Italy, Spain and France and said that maybe I could go with her and her sister. My heart was pounding at the exciting thought, but I didn't know if I should ask Harvey if he would finance the trip. The price for two weeks would be the same as the price for sending both of us to Hawaii for one week, so I thought I would ask.

Harvey and Lori know that travel is educational, so they thought it would be fine for me to go. I was flying on cloud nine!
All the family members and mother-in-law promised to take turns staying with Bumper, so I was free to go!

Getting a passport, packing, and the anticipation of the trip, made the weeks fly! While I would be in Europe, Melvin would keep the shop open.

As happy as I was, I was also sad, because I would be going away, having fun, and Bumper would have to stay home, as usual. He wanted me to go and see the world, so with his blessings, I felt better.

At the airport I met Maggie's sister, Lavern, a banker's wife from North Dakota. I expected a rich, snooty woman, but when I first spotted her running down the concourse, blue jeans and checked shirt, carry-on bag flopping all over the place, looking as though she had been through a tornado, I knew we would get along just fine!

Our group consisted of 80 people, all from the upper Midwest. Seventy-nine Catholics, and one Lutheran.

Harvey warned me that it was a religious trip, and was making sure I knew that. That wouldn't stop me from enjoying my the vacation. Our first destination was Oberammergau, in the Bavarian Alps of Germany, to see the Passion Play. The bus trip up into the mountains scared me, because I am afraid of heights. I tried not to look out the window at the beautiful scenery, because my fear was greater than the beauty. I would enjoy the majestic sights when the bus stopped.

Our group was large. Some stayed in Oberammergau, and the rest of us went to Garmisch, a small town higher up in the mountain. The Bavarian Inn we stayed in was beautiful. Taking a shower was the first thing on my mind; sharing a bath down the hall didn't impress me. They had no towels, so I dried myself with my dirty clothes. I called the desk and complained that the door didn't lock. "No need to worry here. We don't need locks," was the answer. The windows had no screens; I could lean out and enjoy the view. Bavaria was good for me. I forgot about all the medical, health and money problems at home.

The Passion Play the next day was wonderful, it was done in German. Everyone in the play must be life long residents of the town.

In Oberammergau, I purchased cuckoo clocks for the kids and Bumper, which meant I had to haul the darn things all over Europe. I should have listened to the shopkeepers' advice and had them sent home.

Maggie, Lavern, and I enjoyed a delightful lunch on a sidewalk cafe in Munich while we listened to the music of the glockenspiel. The problem of how to pay for lunch was solved when we held out our hands and let the nice, plump, waitress take what she needed. We still had some Deutschmarks left, so we felt pretty good.

I began to realize that Lavern was flighty. She could wander away, and get lost walking around a phone booth. If we had spotted a pet shop, we would have bought a leash.

Next stop, Rome! Our two busses stopped for a tour of the Oblate Mission. From the rooftop, you could see the Seven Hills of Rome. While they all went to Mass, I stayed up on the roof to enjoy the sights of the city. I took a few pictures, then my camera quit. I changed the batteries and it still wasn't working. For the rest of the trip I shared Maggie's camera. Sitting on that rooftop-overlooking Rome, I felt I was the most blessed person on earth. Without Harvey and Lori, I wouldn't be seeing these things. I felt like a millionaire!

The Pope was giving a mass at St. Peter Square. I never dreamed I would ever see the Vatican, or the Pope. We were joined by millions of people, jammed in to the square like sardines. What if I had had to go to the bathroom? I didn't know how they could handle a medical emergency if one arose, with such a large crowd. We stood there a long time before the Pope appeared. I only got a fleeting glance of him as he went by. I was not prepared for such a long Mass, given in five languages.

It was wonderful to see the Pope. I knew that given the chance, I would not go to another Mass! Finding a bathroom was the most important thing on the agenda, which was not an easy chore. When we did find one, the wait was almost as long as the Pope's Mass.

We toured the Sistine Chapel on our own. I expected it to be small, but the many large rooms surprised me. We saw all the beautiful artwork, and looked for Laverne, killing two birds with one stone. She stumbled right onto my feet, breaking a sandal, so I had to go barefoot until we found a shoe store. The pavement was hot. Lavern was a nut. I was thirsty and hungry, and we had trouble finding the bus!

Our hotel was nice, but the food was not good. They served all of us the same thing and it wasn't Italian! (Here in Italy) Maggie had a temper tantrum about the food, went to her room, ordered room service, and when they brought it, she signed the bill 'Pope John.' I don't know who paid the bill, as nothing was ever said.

The next day, we saw the catacombs, Trevi Fountain and the artwork in the churches.

What an education! I learned that the cab drivers do not understand you until you tell them off in English, and then they will tell you off, using different words in our language.

Next stop, Isle of Capri. I loved it! Sorrento, I bought a music box.

I didn't know what country Pomeii was in, so it was a real thrill getting to see the ruins. I had heard about it, but then, I was there!

The bus took us to Monte Cassino, sight of one of the World War II battles. Our sweet Italian guide was very quick to tell about OUR troops (American) bombing the castle on the hill. I don't think he liked us.

We flew to Madrid on what must be the worst airline in the world. It was an old noisy tub that loaded from both back and front, pick your own seat.

Our group toured Madrid, and then on to Toledo, known for its art. In Avilla, a beautiful little walled village, I toured by myself, while all the Catholics went to mass. By skipping church I was able to see more of the towns.

From Madrid our bus took us across the Pyrenees Mountains which were beautiful, if not more so, than the Alps. I thought I had been scared of the roads in the Alps, but now I was terrified. Having several Catholic priests, three nuns in white robes and me, a Lutheran, sent on this trip by my wonderful sister and brother-in-law of Jewish faith, I knew I had all bases covered if we went over a cliff.

Lourdes is a beautiful quaint little village high in the Pyrenees. It has a warmth and stillness that cannot be captured, no matter how many pictures are taken of it. The bridges and streams through the town, the people, the mountains, all this beauty, made it appear like a place in your dreams.

Lourdes is known for its healing water in the grotto, where the virgin appeared to some children. People come in stretchers and wheel chairs to take a bath in the spas. I wanted holy water to bring to Bumper, so I had brought my own large thermos from home.

The first night in Lourdes, I joined all the Catholics in a candle light procession, down a big round drive which goes to the Basilica. I was sure the line was heading to the grotto behind the church, to get holy water. We were given candles, and everyone walked slowly, chanting and singing. The sounds reverberating through the mountains were enchanting. When we got to the Basilica the line I was in walked right past it. "What is wrong, why aren't we going to the grotto?' I said to Maggie. She laughed and said, "We are not going to the grotto, we are saying our beads."

I was walking around in those circles and not getting to the grotto? I got out of that line, and walked around town by myself instead.

While the Catholics were in Mass the next morning, I found my way to the Grotto, filled my jugs and drank from the well. Being the only Lutheran in a Catholic town has its rewards. Everyone complained of the long lines at the Grotto after the mass. It felt good being one step ahead of them.

On the plane heading home, I said a prayer of thanks for a much needed and wonderful vacation. I could face my problems at home refreshed!

Arriving home, Cog didn't want me in the house and Bumper and Heidi were using paper plates, because there were no clean dishes. Bandit was mad at me for leaving, and the only food in the house was a T.V. dinner.

Bumper was happy I was back! "We should take your pictures to be developed," said Bumper. "The camera broke, so we will get doubles of Maggie's' pictures," was my reply. He looked at the camera and said, "The batteries are in backwards."

MR. AND MRS. LEWIS

When Bumper and I were married, we lived in North Minneapolis. Bumper answered the phone one day, and told me that a man was coming out that night, to show us something that could do everything, except maybe paint the house. That was my first hint that Bumper was gullible to salesmen. When the phrase was coined "there's a sucker born every minute," Bumper makes up for ten minutes. I said, "The guy sells vacuum cleaners." He said, " I don't think it's a vacuum." I stared him down and said, "We'll see, he's not coming in the door."

When the doorbell rang, I opened the door to a nice looking man, who seemed sincere. I said to him, "you talked to my gullible husband, but I'm not like him. I know you are selling vacuum cleaners, and I don't need one. We're moving in a week, Please don't bother us." I shut the door in his face.

One week later, we moved into the little house in Zimmerman that Bumper and grandpa had built for us. A few days after we moved in, I was out in the yard when a car came by, "You just move in?" this nice looking man said to me. I looked at him, looked again, and said, "You are the guy I threw out of my house last week". He stared at me and said, "You're right." We both laughed, and that started our lifetime friendship with Mr. and Mrs. Lewis. He brought over his red headed Irish wife to meet us and our friendship was cemented together at that point.

Mr. Lewis didn't sell just one kind of vacuum cleaners, he sold anything and everything. He was so good, he could have had a job with a big company as the super salesman, but he never wanted that, because it would be too easy. He loved the challenge of selling door-to door and he was top dog. It becomes a real game with these guys to see who's the best. It wasn't always door to door, just something that would be impossible, for anyone but a super salesman.

At the Lewis' house, I discovered they hadn't unpacked their wedding gifts from ten years ago. Mrs. Lewis said, "We move so often, why bother?"

They were our neighbors for the next six years, which was the longest they had stayed in one house. The two little red-haired boys were adorable, and reminded me of Dennis the menace, both in looks and actions. In the spring, the two boys had gotten new winter jackets on a clearance sale. Those two little imps put on the warm jackets on a hot day, and wouldn't take them off. We next saw them pounding nails into the neighbor's house in their new jackets. Dennis the menace was the right name for both of them.

Bumper worked in construction before he became sick and was laid off in the coldest part of the winter. Mr. Lewis would always take the winter off from work, but when they needed money, he would go and sell something and share the booty.

After the school bus left, Bumper and I would take the toboggan and slide down the road to the lake, landing almost at Lewis' door. The kids could slide on that road, because it was steep, and closed for vehicles in the winter. We would spend all day playing cards with them, and climb back up the hill when it was time for the bus. The winters were fun and wonderful. We were together all the time. The first New Years Eve in our new house, would be the first of the next twenty-five spent with Mr. and Mrs. Lewis. We always call each other Mr. and Mrs.; maybe because we are even closer than a first name basis. We just started doing it!

We were in a shopping mall one day, and Mr. Lewis ran over to me and said, "Hide me behind you, that guy over there will kill me if he sees me." I protected him with my body, and Bumper stood in the way of the man's vision. We found out that Lewis had sold him something that wasn't a good deal. He did expect that a few people wanted to kill him on sight, if they had the chance.

Soon after that, our dearest and best friends moved. They have moved many times, but we have managed to stay life long friends, and still spend weekends at each other's house. When Bumper was sick, we still spent time with them, and we were always together for New Years Eve. I sure missed having those two living near us.

Instead of a normal job Mr. Lewis needed a challenge, to be his own boss, so he kept moving on, a way of life that suited him.

RANDY'S WEDDING

Soon after Sonja's wedding, Kitty and Randy decided they should be married. Randy thought hen pecking meant love.

We were all hoping our thoughts about this marriage were wrong, but deep down, I knew this love match wasn't made in heaven.

A Justice of the Peace in the Minneapolis Court House married Randy and Kitty, with only the wedding party attending.

Her dad hosted the reception at a church basement. Her mother-step/mother-in-law, and Randy's father-/stepfather-in-law were not there, to witness the marriage of the step-brother, to his step-sister.

Kitty pushed the cake into Randy's face, which didn't sit well with me, but then, who am I?

It was a short, bittersweet affair. We all went there with heavy hearts.

All we could do was to pray that things would be good for them. Bumper had married a woman with four kids and a big dog. I'm sure his family had some doubts about our wedding too.

BUMPER AND THE DOCTOR

Getting Bumper to the doctor was the hardest chore I have ever had. The doctor never gave him wonderful news, like his heart had improved and he was fine, or something he wanted to hear. He was so bad, that I was supposed to give him Valium before he went, or he wouldn't go. One time, I had to give him six - 5-milligram Valium, to get him into the car. I called Dr. Azzam, and he said, "just get him here, I can take care of that when I see him".

When we got to the North Memorial Clinic, he would not go into the office to wait. I told the desk clerk that the bravest patient they have is sitting out by the elevators, facing the elevators, so he won't have to look at the hospital. Dr. Azzam had put him in the hospital a number of times, so he was afraid of that, too. Since there are no benches or chairs by the elevator, Bumper sat right down on the floor. I thought he should sit there and suck his thumb if he wanted to look so stupid. The only thing missing was a pacifier and a diaper.

The nurses knew where to find him, so they came to get him when the doctor was ready. If he had had to sit in the room to wait for the doctor, he would have gone bananas.

Bumper always wore the same clothes to see the doctor: same shirt, same pants, same socks and the same shoes. He even had the underwear marked so he would wear the same pair. After a couple of years, I was embarrassed to take him. Doc must have thought the poor guy had nothing else to wear. When they started to look very shabby, I got rid of all of them. Was I in trouble!

Bumper carried on like he had lost his best friend, which worried me, because he seemed to be losing control. He was determined not to go to the doctor, because he thought that without his charmed clothes, he would certainly die, right in the office. Dealing with his superstition was like trying to move a mountain.

I slipped him a few Valium, got out the new duds, and he did get dressed, but was not a happy camper. He's not too pleasant any time when he has an appointment, so I wasn't too upset about his silly disposition.

Even though he wore his new attire, he came out alive. They didn't stick him in the hospital, so I was forgiven for trashing his special "going to the doctor" clothes.

Each visit was stressful for both of us, what a relief when the appointments were over.

On the way home, he was always his jolly old self, because he was done with the doctor.

UNTIL NEXT TIME!!

CHRISTMAS IN JULY

I thought it would be fun to have a family re-union, since I hadn't invited Bumper's relatives to our small habitat very often. I decided to do something to surprise all of them, our kids, all-living away from home, included. Why would I do something as mundane as a simple picnic?

I called everyone, telling them to come out for dinner on a certain Sunday. They all thought they were the only ones coming. In the "beginning", I couldn't tell Bumper what I was doing, because he often would say that I do strange, crazy things. I thought I would save that fight for later. The battle wouldn't last long, because, when I won, the fight would be over, and it wouldn't take long.

I let my customers know I needed a Santa Suit, and some nice man offered me the use of his. I needed Christmas lawn decorations, so different neighbors loaned them to me. I ordered a Christmas cake, cleaned the house, and the junk I didn't want, I put into Santa's big gift bag. What I needed now was a Santa Claus, to fill the red suit. I thought a couple of minutes, before I decided that Pastor Tom would be perfect! Knowing I am a little different, he thought the idea was great and agreed to be Santa!

Bumper was not too thrilled about this whole idea, but let me have my fun. I hung Christmas stockings in the living room, put up the artificial tree, and then, except for no snow, it looked like Christmas.

The guests started to arrive, and some of the kids were first. They could not believe I had a snowman in the front yard, along with other figures. I could just hear them saying, "Mom is going off the deep end, I think she needs a doctor."

Mother-in-law, Bumper's sister Leslee, husband Bob, and their three boys, which I always called #1,#2, and #3, arrived, and started laughing. Bumper's family sometimes thought I was weird, and I now wanted to give them the benefit of the doubt.

Bumpers Aunt and cousins came, and by then, I was having a ball, just seeing the reactions. It was about 98 degrees that day, but everyone piled into the tiny house, with a window air-conditioner, to admire the tree and Christmas stockings hung with care. The aroma of the turkey and pumpkin pies added to the holiday.

Everyone was enjoying themselves, when a car pulled into the driveway, with a jolly man in a red suit and beard behind the wheel.

Santa and his big sack came into the house, and he was the love of the party. Doesn't everyone have the desire to sit on Santa's Lap? Of course! Poor Santa must have been very hot in that heavy suit, hat and beard.

From his big bag, gifts were given to all, and some didn't seem to like the rubbish that much, but what the heck, it belonged to them, and they had to take it home with them. It was my house; so I could make the rules, and that was my first rule, take home your junk. (gifts)

Included in the debris was an old ugly vase, unmatched socks that I put together as pairs, unmatched silverware, and all kinds of unusual things.

Santa stayed for a while, but I know he was relieved when the guests all had their treasures, and he could depart to his air-conditioned car.

The Party was a huge success, but no one except maybe some of our own kids, and I even doubt that, would have dared to do it, and give away all that worthless trash.

The Party was written up in the Zimmerman Newspaper social column. Nonabelle (the editor) thought our celebration was better news then someone's medical history, procto's and all.

Pastor Tom called me the next day and told me that one little boy went running down the street near our house yelling, "Mom Ma, Mom Ma, I just saw Santa Claus."

THE ARRIVAL OF DANIEL AND MERRI

Two new members entered our family about the same time. Randy and Kitty had a darling boy, Daniel, born April 30th, 1985, the cutest little bundle our first grandchild. The parents loved that baby dearly, but I still had reservations about the marriage. It wasn't made in heaven! Daniel was a rolly polly blonde haired little bundle of love.

Merri, on the other hand, was not born into our family, but she made a big entrance. Jon had a girlfriend! I had given up on that day ever happening, but it did. I knew if Jon found a girl, he would love her completely. Jon loved to get me going, or to put me on about something, and most of the time it worked.

I didn't meet Merri face to face the first time; she called me on the phone. I was listening to her, and she kept my attention. I whispered to Bumper, "She is exactly like Jon!" She was putting me on about meeting her, and how great she was. Trying everything to test my temper. I knew my son was behind this phone call, so I couldn't help laughing! We must have talked, or maybe I just listened for about half an hour. She said I would get the chance to meet her soon.

I hung up the phone and sat and laughed. Bumper wanted to know about the conversation, and through my laughter, I told him, "She's perfect for Jon. If it hadn't been a girls voice, I would have sworn it was him."

I was looking forward to the meeting, because how could anyone not like a girl that would call her boyfriend's mother, sight unseen, try to get her mad and tease her. Most would try to be on their very best behavior, but Merri didn't try to impress me. Merri was Merri, the clone of my son. I knew he had picked the right one without a face-to-face meeting. She would fit in to our family nicely.

BODYGUARD

Bumper was not happy staying home by himself, so it was decided he would go to work with me. He already had the title of shop manager, but couldn't manage, so now he would be called my bodyguard, and he wasn't good at that either. It made both of us seem important! He could sleep in the barber chair if he didn't snore, and keep track of all the excitement in town when he was awake.

I felt better having him there, because I wouldn't have to phone for an ambulance, because the crew was usually in the shop.

He listened to Ray and me banter about which of us would meet the most famous people in our lifetime. We were batting 0! She had met the mayor of Princeton, and I had met Benchwarmer Bob. We both knew the Mayor of Zimmerman. We were not doing well!

We both had dreams of meeting important people, maybe even movie stars. Sometimes dreams come true, sometimes not. If we sat in this little town forever, I didn't feel either of us had a chance of winning this dream game.

Until either of us met someone famous, we would have to settle for our backgammon game. I hated Ray! She would always win because of cheating, but would never own up to it. She wouldn't even start a new game, so I babied her and let her keep winning, just to keep the peace. When she played a game with Bumper, she would always lose, because she only cheated with me!

I soon became known not only as the barber with my own ambulance crew, but also, the barber with my own bodyguard. I think if Ray wanted to meet someone important, she wouldn't have had to look far!

T

HE GOAT OF MANY COLORS

Pastor Tom was leaving our small church for a big congregation in Roseville. (a suburb of St. Paul) We didn't want him to leave. It was decided that anyone who would like to join in some fun on his last Sunday, would bring livestock and tie them in the front yard of his house on the church property. Our idea was that he couldn't leave with all the animals. At least, we could make his leaving a little more bearable by doing this.

Not living on a farm was not going to stop me. I would rent an animal. I thought a goat of many colors would be appropriate, because of the "Coat of many colors," from the Bible story of Jacob's coat. I checked around to see if there were goat farms in the area, and Bumper and I found one, quite a ways out of town.

Bumper felt stupid going with me to talk to the owners of the goat farm, but then, he was used to me. I don't think they had ever had a request to rent a goat, especially one that had to be all white. Pure white! He had a nanny goat I could rent for twenty five dollar a day, and the cost was in my budget so I told him I would pick the goat up early Sunday morning. That farmer never asked me why I needed a goat, but since I would return it later, he couldn't have thought I would use it for a sacrificial offering.

In the car Bumper calmly said, "How are you going to pick up a goat in a car? How do you know you won't be afraid of the goat once you get it?" he added. Neither or those questions had crossed my mind yet, but I would figure something out.

The next day, Wesley, the owner of a trucking company, who was a member of our church, came in for a haircut. I told him my plight about the white nanny goat, and he said he would take me in his pickup truck to get the goat. I could take him home to my backyard to put on his beautiful multi colored coat, and he would come back and pick me up before the second service when all the animals would appear.

That answered Bumper's first question, but the second question would not have an answer until the goat was in my possession. If I could tackle a big turkey, could a goat be much worse?

Sunday morning dawned bright and beautiful, and Wesley picked me up to travel the several miles to get the goat. That calm farmer still didn't inquire about why a goat was needed. If someone wanted an animal of mine, I would want to know why.

It helped that Wesley was a farmer, along with having a trucking company, because he knew something about animals. He got the goat into the pickup. When we arrived at our place, he tied up the goat in the back yard and left the goat to bond with me.

I carefully made all the beautiful colors with food coloring. Blue, green, purple, red, yellow, pink. Then I took a medium size paintbrush, and went to work on Nanny a.k.a. Joseph. She was a good little goat, and stood nicely while her white coat was transformed into a beautiful array of colors. Bumper was his normal useful self by staring out the window to call for help if the goat should decide to start high kicking like he was in the dance line at Radio City Hall. I was proud of nanny when I finished. I was even starting to like the goat! Bumper didn't want to get involved in this project, other than looking out the window. Wesley was right on time, and stood looking at my artwork. "That is a colorful goat there. I've never seen one like it," he said with a big smile.

The goat was back in the truck for the ride to church.

When we got there with Nanny, already there were: a cow, horse, and chickens in cages, rabbits, and a good assortment of animals. When Pastor Tom, and his wife Joanne, emerged from church, they stood in stunned silence at the barnyard. Tom and Joanne started laughing and said "This won't keep me here you know." First service churchgoers also came out and admired the circus, and laughed at the barnyard on the church's property. Tom knew the others were farmers, but was puzzled about the ownership of the goat. He knew I had brought it, but also knew I didn't own one. I told him, "I have rented it, but if you will stay, I will buy it." They were laughing hard now. I didn't' know if it was because the goat was so colorful, or because I had rented one. I was about to go into church, when Pastor Tom's dog decided he hated that goat, and tried to attack it. Some kind people put the dog in the house, so the goat would be safe during the church service.

What I didn't know, was that Pastor Tom had arranged for someone to steal the goat, and hide it. He had found someone before the service, so he worked fast to get even with me. Coming out of church I had no goat! I thought Pastor Tom had played a part in the missing goat mystery, but would not admit to anything. Many thoughts raced through my head on the way home. How much will the goat cost to replace if it is lost? When Bumper found out, he became very nervous.

Not much I could do. Where would you look for a goat? I figured if Tom had a part of this, I would find out sometime soon, because he knew that Bumper couldn't take much stress.

I was right! A couple hours later, Pastor Tom told me where to pick up the colorful nanny. Recruiting the pick up again, we got the goat and took her back to the farm. Bumper and I followed the pickup, because Bumper wasn't going to miss the farmer's face when the world's most beautiful goat returned.

Wesley put Nanny in the fence with the many off color goats, and MY goat stuck out! You could spot Nanny in a second. The farmer came out, looked, stared, looked, and stood and laughed. He then got the story on his "holy" goat, the only one in the bunch to have gone to church! He laughed so hard, I didn't have to pay rental on Nanny. He was proud of her coat!

CHICAGO

Some friends of mine were driving to Chicago for the weekend and asked if I would like to ride along. They would drop me off at Lori's house in Kenilworth. Lori was alone in their mansion on the lake, while Harvey was in Oxford, England, studying Shakespeare, so I thought she might like the company. Bumper liked the idea of two sisters spending time together, so we arranged for the family to check in on him. Lori was happy to hear I was coming. The car was a tiny little sports job, so the back seat was crowded with just my body, but that was fine.

My sister's fortress was protected about as well as the U.S. Mint. It didn't surprise me when the alarms sounded before I had been in the house three minutes. I was picturing the police surrounding the house and talking to me through a P.A. system. My vision included s.w.a.t. teams coming through the door with guns blazing. My life passed before me. There was no evil deed, just a few good ones I hadn't performed yet. Lori ran through the place, having eight seconds to disarm the system. She said, "I knew you would do that".

The big living room looked like a funeral home, with the casket missing. The spooky elevator with the front and back staircases should have been in a mystery movie. Once I was in bed for the night, I didn't move. No way would I wander about that house after dark.

Lori asked what I would like to do while in the windy city. I told her, but she said "no" to my idea, which was to window peek in all the surrounding mansions. No sense of humor that girl! In that area you don't stop by for a chat, you must be invited in.

We did do some quick shopping, because Lori doesn't approve of my wardrobe.

After our swim in the indoor pool the next morning, we started off for a tour of the Botanical Gardens. The 90+-degree heat didn't dampen the beauty of all the wonderful flowers. Oh the fragrance! We got on the tram to go further into the preserve. I had to chuckle on this trip, because it took us through prairie grass, same as we have at home pine trees and weeds that grow like those in my yard. I suppose when you live in the melting pot, you see nothing of the country, even a cow, unless you go to the zoo. My sister paid money to show me what I have in my own back yard. Makes sense! Knowing how important these weeds and grasses are will make me view my own with awe and admiration, and possibly a subpoena from the Sheriff for keeping noxious weeds. A couple of years ago, Bumper's grandma came over, and asked me why I had my "favorite plant." "Because it's beautiful and grows like a weed," I said. "It is a damned weed," she said, "It's itch weed". That plant was growing up around the windows and I loved it. It was the only plant that didn't need much care or fertilizing. I didn't take Grandma's advice; I kept it for a few more years.

That night, we ate K.F.C. chicken in her garden at the mansion. I am a slow eater, so dinning with Lori was an experience. My plate was half full and she said, "Let's go," "Where are we going"? "To the movie"," she said. She told me how hard it is to eat with Harvey, because he eats so fast, she can't keep up with him. I think they are like two peas in a pod!

The next morning after our swim, we went shopping. I like that as much as peeking in the mansion windows. On the way to shopping, we went through town, and I peeked in the two barbershops. The barbers make a ton of money, the customers come up in limos, and the shops are ordinary. My own is much nicer. The town is so rich, that garbage trucks are not allowed in, because they do not want the noise. Pick up trucks are used for the trash. You don't see residents in the yard, only the gardeners. Crime is not a problem, because crooks don't dare enter. Shopping was great, because she bought shoes to go with each outfit. Between her taking me shopping, and the packages of clothes Lori would send to me, I was living right!

Back at my sister's fortress, I called Bumper and told him that I had a Liz Claiborne collection. He said, "Who's she?" Fashion to him is getting a pair of colored underwear for Easter.

We went to an outdoor production of ANNIE GET YOUR GUN. It was great. Lori's driving was awful. The parking was limited, so she pulled up on the curb, parked where nothing should be parked, and left it. Oh well, that's my sister! I was surprised it was still there after the play. Because of her excellent parking, it was easy to find!

In the morning Lori told me there was a tour through some of the mansions; given by her women's club. I loved seeing those huge mansions. High tea was at her exclusive club. I was wearing black. I picked out things full of powdered sugar, and I was a mess! My black dress was now white and wouldn't brush off. I felt like a bull in a china shop. How could those women eat the same thing, and not be messy? Lori acted like she didn't know me. I was glad of that! I felt sorry for her.

In the basement of this mansion, they have a storeroom that is bigger than our house. We went down there and Lori said, "if you see something you need, grab it" It was like turning me loose at Target.

When my friends came to pick me up in the compact car, they just stared at all the things I had accumulated to take back home with me. "No way will all that fit in the car," they said. Lori laughed and said, "I can get it all in there with no problem," and she did. It was uncomfortable sitting on top of things, no room for my legs, but I did it for almost eight hours.

Getting home, I needed help to get out of the car, I could barely move. Cog growled at me for one hour, as I was trying on each outfit for Bumper at that late hour. The cat ignored me.

Sleeping with a hot water bottle helped my aching joints. Working with the pain was not easy. Ray saw my new wardrobe, and soon, everyone in town knew about my pink shoes and purple shoes.

ARRIVAL OF MERRI AND WILLIE

Merri entered into our lives by making an appearance with Jon in the barbershop. The minute she opened her mouth, I felt like I had known her forever. I was positive that she would be part of our family some day, because she was perfect for my son. Merri was as tall as our 6 foot two son. Her long auburn hair and beautiful smile could make anyone melt.

She didn't try to impress us; just being her self did that. Bumper and I found her to be a joy to be around. She believed in laughter, and made everyone around her feel good. What more could my son want? I was thinking that maybe I should start planning for the groomsmen dinner, but on second thought, I decided to wait until Jon proposed to her. I knew someday he would.

I also had the joy of meeting Willie that day. In walked this cute, young man from town that had been to Molar Barber School, but found it very hard to do his apprenticeship in the twin cities. An apprentice doesn't make much money, and it was a long way to drive. He had a working wife and two kids. Remembering my apprentice days I felt sorry for him. I told I didn't need anyone else, but if he didn't mind not making a lot of money, I would get him through his apprenticeship. He was happy with that, so he became part of the shop. No one in his or her right mind would take on someone that wasn't needed, but what the heck, I didn't want to be stuck into a normal way of a life anyway. Willie was a good barber, so I didn't have the need to teach him much. He was, I believe the only apprentice to have a key to the shop where he worked, and I am sure the only one to figure out how much money he earned each week, and could pay himself. I knew he was honest, so I didn't worry about it. He liked working with me.

I think I was the only shop owner to let everyone pay themselves I pride myself in being a good judge of people and business.

CHRISTMAS IN THE BARBER SHOP

Christmas in the Barbershop was an exciting time of year. The smell of coffee, hot cider and fresh evergreen, would greet you when the door opened.

Each year, I would buy the biggest, fresh tree I could find. Also I would run an ad in the local paper about the ornament contest. The children in the community were invited to enter, with three different age groups, to make a tree ornament. In each group, there was a first, second, and third prize for the best. Kids of all ages put their hearts into making the decorations, and they were wonderful. Some ornaments were beautifully made so it was hard to believe they could do it themselves.

Each child would come in with a proud smile, check that their name was written on the ornament, and pick a place for it on the tree.

Just before Christmas, the tree would be loaded onto a pickup truck, for the short ride to the senior citizens apartment building. The residents would stand waiting for it to arrive. After all the oohs and aahs, they would sit down, pick up each ornament, and after a full day or two, take a vote on which ones would be the lucky winners of cash prizes. They would let me know which children were on the list, and I would call them and tell them to come for the money. It was known as the CHILDREN'S CHRISTMAS TREE, and became more popular each year.

The children could pick up their ornaments at the apartment building if they would like to keep them. They were as beautiful as anything you could buy in a store. They would be treasures to keep forever.

SOCIAL SECURITY

In 1983, Social Security Disability had a bad year. They weren't the only ones. The infinite wisdom of the people that make the decisions, decided they would take everyone off, and start all over. The very sick and disabled were taken off, as well as those that were faking and cheating the system. I know something needs to be done about the misuse of government funds, but that made no sense.

At the time a small portion of my husband's heart was working. He was told by a letter from the Social Security office that he should go to work. Ridiculous! His check was needed, as it had to buy all off his prescription medicines, that Social Security did not cover. I got an attorney, and like everyone else, wondered how we would pay the legal fees.

It was a bad four months while we were without his check: The doctor still wanted his bill to be paid, the medicines couldn't wait, nor could the lights, gas, or telephone. The pharmacist and utility companies didn't care that Social Security was having problems.

It was so ridiculous that I ran a couple of ads in our local paper, which I shall keep forever. Since Social Security said he should work, I wanted to see if anyone would hire him. Here's the text of the ad I ran --

"Wanted--Job. Can only work three hours a day. $25.00 an hour. No lifting. No heavy work. No standing more than a few minutes. No stress. No arm work. Indoor only. No work when below zero, or hot and humid. Air-conditioning a must. No more than one mile from Zimmerman. Complete medical coverage is necessary. Twenty days per year sick leave. Experienced in high steel-Fire-fighting Military: If Hiring call Frontier Office."

A lot of people called about getting that job, but no one called that needed that job filled.

Our Attorney saw the ad, laughed, hung it in his office, and decided that the government was so stupid, that he would take on our case for nothing!

When things would get stressful, I would try to do something to make Bumper laugh, so I ran another ad: For Sale-Black Tom Cat (neutered). Very independent. Likes special diet and eats with family. Needs own room, but sleeps with people. $3500.00 (that is hundred) New owners must be inspected and approved by present parents. No children allowed, because cat doesn't care for them, now that our kids have grown. Cat must have at least one person home most of the time.

Bumper almost went bonkers when he saw the ad. Bandit was HIS, and he was madder than a junkyard dog. I was laughing while explaining to him that no one would want the cat. Even if we gave it away, no one in their right mind would want a spoiled black tomcat! I had our phone number listed with the newspaper, so each day, he would live in fear that someone would want to buy a thirty-five hundred dollar cat! I said, "If they are dumb enough to call, we don't have to approve of them." I think he felt better knowing that.

The cat brought us no money, but we didn't want any gained by selling him. Bumper didn't think it was a funny joke!

The battle with the government lasted over three months. Bumper was put back on social security with statements from many doctors. Social Security wanted him to go to their own doctor, but Dr. Azzam, one of the best, fought tooth and nails. He said, "What would you do for testing his heart?" They replied, "Give him a chest x-ray." Get serious! That was the bureaucrats sending a heart patient to a General Practitioner, who can't get a job in a hospital. I think he graduated 50th, in a class of 50.

Even with our attorney fighting, we did not get any back pay! They acted like he had never been taken off!

HURRICANE LORI AND THE BLUE CARPET

Jon lived in, and was caretaker, of an upper class apartment building. A tenant had put in a new carpet, and plenty of very nice carpet was left over. There was enough to do our living room and hall. Jon called to see if we would like the beautiful brown carpet that was in excellent condition. Of course we would love it. Our own was very shabby, just like our furniture, and a new carpet would spruce the place up a bit.

A few days before Grumps Big Birthday Bash, Jon delivered it to the house and installed it. I was working at the time, and eager to come home to see the elegant new carpet. Excited!

Jon had already left with the old carpet by the time I got home. Walking in the door, I saw our new treasure. A bright, SKY BLUE carpet! How could a mother ever forget that her son is colorblind? I should not have listened when he told me the color. Stupid, that's what I was.

The only good thing was that this awful color carpet was not shabby. It was clean and expensive, but who in their right mind would buy a carpet this color? Whoever had owned it must have had furniture to match it. Nothing in our house matched. It's hard to match early Halloween decor, but the carpet showed us how bad the furniture was.

Lori was coming the next day for Grandpa's birthday party, which would be in two days, and here I was with this monstrosity of a carpet. Oh well, she is used to me. Bumper, of course, was admiring the damn thing, and he's not color blind. It will be Ok if I close my eyes going through the living room.

The kids brought Lori out from the airport the next day. Like I said, she is used to me, so she was carrying a suitcase full of things to redo the bathroom; wallpaper, shower curtain, curtain, throw rugs and mat, soap dish and toothbrush holder. She looked at the carpet and decided she had more work to do.

When she is doing a project, I stay out of her way, because one should never walk head on into a hurricane. I hide, the kids hide, and Bumper becomes invisible. She spent most of the night doing the bathroom. Hurricanes don't sleep.

Jon spent the weekend with us, so very early the next morning, Lori woke Jon and Heidi and told them she had a job for them to do. Mumbling under their breath, they got up to find out what was in their aunt's mind.

"Start throwing all the living room furniture out in the yard. Add the kitchen table and chairs too." she said. The kids looked at each other, then at me. They thought Lori was cracking up for sure. They knew better than to argue with her, so they started lifting it all into the yard.

When Bumper came on the scene, he was pretty mad, because that old ratty couch and chair were his favorite things in the house. I have to admit that they were awful, and I didn't feel bad about them being tossed out into the yard.

Leaving all the furniture in the yard for the neighbors to wonder about, we went to set up for Grandpa's party.

That night, after the party, we sat around on the blue carpet and had a little gab session. Lori said before she went to bed, "We have to leave early for the airport, because we have to buy furniture on the way."

The next morning we left for the airport, and Bumper was standing admiring the new carpet as we left. In the city, we stopped at a large furniture chain store where Lori picked out everything new for the living room, plus a kitchen table and chairs.

While we were gone, Bumper called Ray and told her to get the crew to come and pick up a bunch of furniture from our yard. The big ambulance barn was rather empty, so they could use couches and anything that was thrown their way.

The new furniture was delivered the next day and the blue carpet still looked bad, but with the new things, it didn't look QUITE as bad.

Bumper did not like the new couch and chairs. The chairs were the same blue as the carpet and looked good. He didn't like the couch, because it wasn't the same as the old worn out one. He didn't like the recliner, because he was used to the one with the holes right where his elbows hit the chair. He missed the old junk.

It is hard to change a stubborn old dog to new things.

NON-JEWISH MOTHER

My Jewish son-in-law always told me that I was the most non-Jewish, Jewish mother he had ever encountered. He thought I always meddled into their affairs, but that isn't true.

Randy and Kitty had their second and last child, November 25,1986, a few days before Thanksgiving. A little girl, Kirsten, was adorable with her blue eyes and blonde hair. Kirsten and Daniel both looked like the Norwegian ancestry they were born into.

We were all invited to Sonja's for Thanksgiving dinner, but she got the flu the day before. Of course, I worried about her having the flu. Would her body strong enough to fight it? Marty wasn't mad the first few times I called to check on her fever, but each time I called after that, he seemed to get more business like and polite. He didn't like it one bit when I sent Jon to deliver homemade chicken soup that would help overcome the flu.

I told Marty we wouldn't come for Thanksgiving, because exposing Bumper to the flu would be rather stupid. His sister from Boston was there, so he would have dinner anyway.

The night before thanksgiving, I called all the kids to make sure they would have a place to eat thanksgiving dinner.

Kitty would be coming home from the hospital on Thanksgiving, so Randy would make some food. He laughed at me when I said that they shouldn't take the new baby out and expose her to the flu. He sounded like he thought my brains were dead. I do worry, because none of them are Rhodes Scholars, and sometimes guidance is needed.

If Sonja was better, I thought Heidi should go there since a big bird was being cooked anyway. She wouldn't starve, and would have a place to spend the day. Jon would like McDonalds better than any turkey, but I insisted he go to Sonja's, because they would feel badly about it if only Heidi came from our family. Heidi assured me that all of them had brains enough to figure things out for themselves, that they would all eat and be happy. Still, a mother worries!

Jon had stayed with us a few days before thanksgiving, and Bumper's rash came back. It was a real puzzle, because when Jon was living at home or was between apartments, Bumper broke out in a rash. When he moved, it would disappear. He was only staying this time for a day or so, so the rash didn't last long. I hate to think Bumper is allergic to our son, but he must be! I worried about the rash.

Jon assured me that instead of McDonalds, he would go to Sonja's because, being so macho, the flu did not scare him one bit. He also told me that Marty hadn't appreciated the chicken soup at all. Jon felt that if chicken soup was needed, they could have gone to the store and gotten some much more easily.

After many long distance calls, I had gotten Thanksgiving organized for everyone except Gramps, Bumper and me. The stores were already closed in our small town and I had no turkey. I didn't want to fix one for the three of us anyway! We decided we would pick up Gramps at his apartment and take him out for dinner. We knew the restaurant choices would be limited, but we didn't know the only thing open would be a truck stop. Bumper and Gramps both loved that idea, because they are the truck stop type. I'm not, I go for something a little more elegant like Perkins or Denny's, but what can you do?

Thanksgiving morning, I called Marty to make sure the turkey was in the oven, and to see how my daughter was feeling. He was downright cranky! Maybe something bit him. He assured me that, "Sonja would live. The turkey was roasting in the oven. Everything was under control. Stop worrying, and hang up the damn phone!" I guess that meant he could survive without my help.

I called Randy to make sure everything was OK. Kitty would come home from the hospital, they would eat, and newborn Kirsten was fine. Daniel was fine. Not to worry! I was amazed that things were going so smoothly. I must have taught them well! Not one of them needed me!

We picked up Gramps. At the exclusive truck stop where we ate, those two ninnies (my husband and my father) decided breakfast would be better than a good dinner. I ate turkey. Grandpa wasn't feeling well, so he wanted to go home and take a nap right after dinner. Our truck-stop Thanksgiving will always be remembered.

Anyone who thinks that I act like a Jewish mother has not met my sister. That woman worries about her kids, my kids, her husband, my husband, my kids' jobs, her kids' jobs, her health, my health, everyone's health, Grandpa, her grandchildren, my grandchildren, my weight, my driving, her car, my car, my kids' spouses, her kids' spouses, and anything else she might think of. I know where she got it from, Grandpa! He has worried all his life about everything and solved nothing. I'm glad I don't take after those two.

The only thing that makes Lori the un-typical Jewish Mother, is that fact that she can't make chicken soup or chopped liver. Me, the non-Jewish mother? NEVER!

HALFTRACK

Christmas has always been my favorite time of year. In 1986, Christmas started a few weeks early when I received a package in the mail from mother-in-law, who lived in Florida during the winter months.

The package was addressed to me, but nosey Bumper decided to open it one day when he had stayed home from the shop. The big chicken opened it up only half way, because he became scared when he saw a brown back. He has always liked to think he is a big strong gorilla that can handle any situation, but he didn't do too well while opening MY Christmas package.

After his dog was done growling at me for coming home, Bumper pointed to a half opened package on the couch. He said, "It's for you." I wondered why it was partly opened, but started to remove the newspapers from the top. As I was taking papers off, I came upon a threatening looking tail. Bumper told me that was as far as he had gone with the unpacking. He said he had decided he didn't want to spoil my surprise, so he didn't finish opening the package. I was thinking of a snake, but the package didn't have holes, so it couldn't be something alive. Even if it was a dead snake, I knew death, for me, would be quick to come. A garden snake would kill me as fast as a cobra, because my heart would stop before it could even bite me. Even a dead one curled up, would be my waterloo!

I asked Bumper if he would finish opening it for me. He pretended to be brave and macho and said that he didn't want to wreck the surprise of whatever might be inside. He thought I should open my own present. Holding Cog, he slinked to the other side of the room and sat down, so that whatever was inside could not get at the master of the house and his royal mutt. The cat, much braver than the mean little dog, had to fend for himself.

My hands were shaking from fright as I pulled off more wrapping paper until I came to a big brown back of some strange animal. I knew it wasn't a snake, but I was extremely curious at this point, but still fearful of what I might find. Using more caution, expecting something to terrorize or bite me, I pulled off more of the paper. I knew the monster had to have a head, again I asked Bumper if he would please open the rest of it, but he couldn't because he had to go to the bathroom. He had, of course, more things to do when he came out of the bathroom, so with no backup support, I had to finish unpacking the monster by myself. I was sure that it was not breathing, because the tail was stiff.

I put my shaking hands around the "things" back, and started lifting this ex life form from another planet out of the tomb that had been its home all the way from Florida.

Bumper did take a look at it after I had gotten it out of the box. I had seen pictures of one in books, but wasn't sure what it was. Bumper spends most of his time looking up un-important things, that no one cares about, so he knew that my present was an armadillo. Now that the fear was gone, I found him to be beautiful. Mother–in-law thought I should have a pet of my own, since Bumper had two. I found a home for him in the corner of the living room, but that home didn't last long. Cog was so stupid; he couldn't tell the difference between something dead or alive, to say nothing about male or female. He wanted to mate with it, and thought it was his private pet. He growled and snapped when I took his love away, but it was MINE! The next day, I bought a rhinestone collar for my wonderful new pet that I named Halftrack. He would have a home forever and be loved.

I took him to the barbershop with me to display the beautiful creature. Most of the customers said they would not want one, even as gift. Some even hated poor halftrack. Bumper ignored him, but Ray and I thought he was perfect. I think that proves that Ray and I have class.

CHRISTMAS 1986

In 1986, we discovered that Grumps had a large tumor on his lung. He had been sick, so I took him to the doctor, against his will. He prided himself in the fact that he hadn't gone to a doctor since World War 11, and that was only for a physical. He didn't like what the doctor told him, but chose not to believe him, so everything was fine. Except for the sickness.

At his apartment, we had a woman come to cook every day supper for him. He thought it was very nice of her to take such good care of him, but he didn't know we were paying her to cook for him, otherwise he would not have eaten.

The apartment staff told us that he was not capable of taking care of himself any longer and belonged in a nursing home. Fortunately, there was a very good one right next to his apartment building. Lori said she would come out over Christmas and get him set up in the nursing home. That was good, then he could hate both of us.

Harvey was in Israel, so Lori decided she would have Subie and her children come too, because it might be Gramps last Christmas. It would also be a first for me, celebrating Christmas with my Jewish family.

I called Subie to tell her how happy we were that they would be coming here for Christmas. " I didn't know we were. When did all this happen?" she asked. I told her about her mom making that decision, and she said that was not unusual for her. She was happy about it too.

Lori arrived on Christmas Eve. In her large suitcase were all sorts of things to redo our bedroom. She also planned on getting someone to build a walk-in closet for us. She had curtains, wallpaper and anything else you want to imagine in her luggage. While we opened the presents, she wanted to do the bedroom, because Christmas was not her thing.

Harvey called that night and surprised Lori with the fact that he was in Turkey trying to get Momo's uncle out of the country. Momo is my niece Kyra's husband, and was born in Israel, which makes him a Sabra. His family came from Turkey, but one uncle was having a problem getting out of Turkey, so Harvey tried to help. Lori was frantic, because that was not a good place for any one to be at that time. We all prayed for his safe return. We found out later that unfortunately he was not able to help the Uncle.

We were to have Christmas dinner in the large party room at Grandpa's apartment building. The kids wanted ham for the meal; Lori's family doesn't eat ham, so we wanted to have turkey also. Grandpa insisted on lutefisk and lefsa. How could we make all that food and get it all from my house to the apartment building? Lori stayed at Grampa's, so I asked her if she would put a turkey in the oven for me. Having her own cook, she had no idea how to do it. "Will you put in a ham then," I asked her? I explained that "a ham is simple, you do nothing except put it in a pan and turn on the oven," She agreed, warily, to do that.

Subie came in early Christmas day, so we were all together for the dinner. It was wonderful! Lori did not screw up the ham, which was a relief to everyone.

Later in the day we discussed with Grandpa about going to the nursing home. He didn't want to, but we told him that it would be good for him for the winter. His cook was going away for the winter, and I couldn't get there every day with food for him. He didn't like the idea, but agreed to it since it would only be for a few months.

Later that day, we went out to our house and munched on all the leftovers. I will never forget my dear sister when she asked for napkins. I didn't have any. "Are there paper towels in the house"? she asked, but I had forgotten to buy some. "I'll go get some toilet paper to use," she said as calm as a cucumber. The richest woman I know would use toilet paper for napkins. That is my sister, and I love her.

The next morning, Lori and I took Grandpa to the nursing home. He didn't throw a fit. When we went back later in the day, he seemed very content. A load had been lifted from our shoulders with him being cared for in such a nice place. We wouldn't have to worry until spring. Then we would face the challenge of gramps wanting to go home.

The next day, before Lori and her family left for home, we were all thankful because we found out that Harvey and Momo were now out of Turkey, and safely back in Israel.

What a wonderful holiday! My winter would be nice, because I wouldn't have to worry about Grampa being by himself. With such a good family, I considered myself blessed, and very wealthy (without money of course).

THE GATHERING STORM

Bumper had a medical appointment the morning of July 23,1987. That morning was just as stressful, getting him to the clinic, as all the rest had been. Valium, fear, valium, bitching…my own nerves were shattering, because Bumper wasn't feeling well; I was trying to stay calm.

I checked him in while he sat on the floor by the elevators bitching because I had thrown out his lucky clothes. Thank God, the wait was short, and so was the appointment. Dr. Azzam found that his heart was working at 5%. That is hardly working at all, and near death. They whisked him off to the hospital, straight from the doctor's office, and the day got worse from then on.

He needed some immediate work done on his heart, and the arteries to be opened, but there was no heart surgeon at North Memorial Hospital that our doctor wanted to do it. He had one in mind, from the transplant team at Abbott Hospital, so he tried to arrange surgery for him early the next morning. In the meantime, he would need emergency surgery. The decision was to install a balloon in the heart, to try to keep him alive until morning. They were instructed not to install a Jarvis, the machine that was used to keep one alive while waiting for a heart, but on which no one had survived so far. Bumper would take his chance on staying alive without one.

The kids all gathered in force, and we made Sonja's home in south Minneapolis our home base. The surgeons would insert a balloon sometime in the late afternoon.

Leaving the car at the hospital, Marty took me home to put Cog into a kennel, since no one would come in and take care of him, because of his temperament.

Wanda, a friend of mine, had tried it once, wearing big gloves, but it didn't work. I felt I shouldn't ask her again. The cat also needed someone to come in and feed him, and give him attention and love. Clothes for me would be nice to have too, but I couldn't think about it now

I found one kennel that would give Cog his own private little cell, and promised to pamper the little pooch. We could drop him off on the way back, since it was on the way. The stress was starting to get to me, but I managed to throw some clothes together.

Marty's car was not air-conditioned, which didn't help ease the situation in the 90-degree heat of the day. My teeth were chattering, but not from the hot day. I knew I could be a widow by morning, and the thought scared me, and sent my mind wandering, where I didn't want it to be.

When we got about twenty-five miles down the road, I screamed at Marty to go back home. I had forgotten something. He told me that if I had clothes, and had found someone to care for the cat, there was nothing more I needed. I was screaming, my face getting beet red, that I needed something and we must turn back. He was just as mad as I was, but I wasn't giving in. Softly talking under his breath, (probably wishing I wasn't his mother-in-law,) he turned the car around and headed back. I didn't want to tell him what I needed until I got there, or he would make another stop at the mental hospital that brought patients to the barber school I had attended.

Tearing into the house, I grabbed the thermos from the dresser and ran back to the car. Marty was fuming as he said, "You needed coffee now"? "No, it isn't coffee, it is water from Lourdes." He didn't believe in Lourdes water, but he hadn't been there. You do not have to be a Catholic to believe in Lourdes, or its water. I needed some to put on Bumper, because if the miracle water was ever a necessity, it was now!

Marty had given up on my sanity. He just put up with me until we arrived at the kennel. Cog was not a happy dog. The kennel keeper asked if there was anything special that he should know about the little adorable dog, who was too nervous to bite me. " No, just give him a lot of love. I'll pick him up in a day or two."

We got back to the hospital and I was cranky and wet from the heat. The balloon would be inserted into his heart very soon. Mother-in-Law and the kids were there waiting for us.

Pastor Tom had moved away, so the new minister came to the hospital. He asked if all our affairs were in order, and told me that I should prepare myself, because there was a chance that he might not make it this time. That was not what I wanted to hear, and I let him know it. He said I wasn't being realistic. He was right, but I would never give up hope. Bumper was not going to leave me. Not now! I did know there was a chance of widowhood for me, but was not going to think about that.

The risky installing of the balloon was finished in a few hours. He was alive, but it would be touch and go through the night. The best surgeon from Abbott Hospital would be at North Memorial Hospital tomorrow morning for a seven A.M. operation. The kids all went back to Sonja's. They would stop and get Chinese food, and would be waiting for us when Sonja and I got there. We both wanted to stay with Bumper a little longer.

That little longer was too long, because all of a sudden, the skies opened up. Thunder and lightning were seen and heard throughout the hospital, and suddenly the lights went out. Emergency lighting kicked in, but this storm wasn't helping to calm our shattered nerves. Could anything else happen?

We heard that the under-passes on the highway were flooding, so we felt we should leave before it got worse. After we drove a few blocks, we could no longer see the road, so Sonja, who was driving my car, pulled into a strip mall, where only two cars were parked. I decided to call Lori. She was tense about Bumper's plight, and since we couldn't drive for the minute, I ran in to call her in Chicago.

Running as fast as I could to get out of the downpour, some idiotic old lady told me, "You can't park in a disabled spot." Her sanity was in doubt, because no one with a sane mind would be standing in a deserted parking lot in a downpour, with tornado warnings, telling someone to move their car. My reply, "Watch me". The torrential rain stopped for a bit, so we started off again, Sonja at the wheel. The sky was an awful looking green color, the most threatening I had ever seen in my life. At the under-passes cars were stalled, because water was up to the motors. The terrible sky, the water and all the stranded cars were frightening. We didn't need the added stress. Sonja was calm, and kept going as fast as she could through the water. Which would be up to our hips if we were outside the car. We felt sorry for all the other cars, but we could not stop, or we would be among them.

I was glad she was driving, because I know I wouldn't have made it through the water, but she did. I know God helped her drive that night, because no one but us made it through the flooded under-passes. It was a terrifying trip, with the rain, ominous sky and my Bumper near death. I knew Sonja had a healthy heart now, because she was the rock! And how I needed her!

The kids were worried about us, knowing we were on the road in such dreadful weather. Relieved when we got home, we sat down and ate the Chinese food, but no one had much of an appetite. Everyone was spending the night there, so Merri, Heidi, Sonja and I, all slept in her huge waterbed, which made me seasick. The boys slept any-place available. The storm was subsiding; but we learned from the radio that almost everyone in the area had flooded basements.

I should have been tired enough to sleep, but the anxiety kept me awake.

THE AFTERMATH

The hot, sleepless and uncomfortable night was over. I decided to go to the hospital in my car, so that later on I could leave for home from there. Those plans didn't work out, however, because the flood we had gone through had left water in the engine, so the car wouldn't start. We heard that many roads were washed out and closed. There were traffic delays everywhere, so getting to the hospital would take longer than expected. I decided to ride with one of the boys.

The surgery would be delayed, because the Doctor would be late getting there due to the roads. (A few more hours of panic and stress.) Oh well! I went to Bumper and put the Lourdes water on him. No one knew if he'd make it through the night, but thankfully he did. I felt God and the holy water had both helped. Even the kids were wondering about me, because they figured the Lourdes Holy water was a Catholic thing and wouldn't work for a Lutheran. Maybe I would make believers out of them.

Two hours later the doctors arrived and the surgery was to start. They would do four bypasses and try to correct the damaged heart. They made no promises to us, but I was expecting miracles. I would not think that God got us through a road where all the cars were stranded except us, to take Bumper away. I just would not think differently. Jon said, "Why don't we just get him a new heart?" I explained that transplant would be in the not so far future. They were the only ones looking forward to a transplant!

I wish the pessimistic minister had been there, because Bumper did live through the surgery, surprising and elating Dr. Azzam.

We stayed to make sure he would be OK, then left because he was hooked up to a big machine and wouldn't know anything for a day or so.

From Sonja's house I started home, and made a stop to pick up Cog. I was happy to be getting him out of the kennel, even though I would have to care for the little beast until Bumper was home again. That dog just did not like anyone except Bumper.

The kennel person was happy to know that the dog would be leaving, but he was angry at me. When I got there, He said, "You didn't tell us he was mean. If he comes again, he will be put in the section with the big mean dogs." The price was different than they had quoted me, because of his temperament. They charged me the "mean" dog prices. I knew Cog was glad to be leaving there, although he didn't kiss me. At least he didn't bite me when they handed him to me with their gloved hands.

In a small town, people really care about one another and try to help in times of trouble. Bumper was becoming the miracle of Zimmerman. To me, with all the bills, he was also becoming the million-dollar man.

Things were getting back to normal even with Bumper gone. The Cat was ignoring me; Cog growled when I looked at him, and I filed all the unopened bills in the trashcan.

NURSING HOME

Grandpa would never let on to any of us that he liked the nursing home, but we knew he didn't hate it as much as he would have us believe. We took him out every Sunday, but as soon as we were done eating, he wanted to go back home, home being the nursing home. He felt secure, and didn't mind being waited on. As far as we knew, he didn't suffer much pain with the lung cancer, but Grandpa would never give in to any pain. I wish we could have known if he was hurting, but he wouldn't discuss his health with us, because he didn't own up to having any problems.

Grandpa took no pills, but he did decide he would like a drink now and then. The nursing home let him have drinks as long as we bought the beer and whiskey. They would keep it in a locked cupboard, and give it to him when he wanted it, as long as he was strapped into a wheelchair. The home was smart in this decision, because the nursing staff could tolerate their job better. Grandpa didn't drive them nuts when he could smoke and drink. Grandpa must have decided that drinking wasn't so bad on the return trip from Arizona, because before that, it never crossed his mind to have a few. Maybe the poor guy was in pain, and drinking the liquor gave him some relief. Maybe he was just bored. I wish we knew the answers, but as long as it would made his last days better, we were all for it.

One morning, the nursing home called me at work and said Grandpa was not doing well. I hurried to get there and found him almost in a state of coma. He lived only a few more hours.

Grandpa was a character, but he had a family that loved and took care of him. He kept our life interesting.

Randy came to the nursing home to see him before they moved him, so he went with me to make the arrangements.

Bumper had been so sick, that trying to work, take care of him, and get to the nursing home to see Grandpa was getting too hard for me. I think God knew that, and took Grandpa fast, to ease the suffering for him and all of us.

On a hot day in the middle of August, Grandpa was laid to rest next to Mom. Bumper couldn't make the funeral because he wasn't doing well. He and Mother-in-Law stopped at the church afterward, just like they had at my Mother's funeral.

Yes, my Dad at times was a pain in the ass, but having a pain in the ass, was better than not having him at all. My sister and I will always love and miss both Mom and Dad.

JON AND MERRI WEDDING

The wedding was to take place in a small church in Anoka, a town near us.

Trouble started right away, because the two kids decided they would have Pizza at the reception. JUST PIZZA! That didn't set well with me, because I didn't think all the relatives coming from a long distance would like to have pizza. Merri's mother was for the idea, so that was a small problem that had to be solved with a certain kind of persuasion. I won! No way would I let all the relatives come to eat pizza. I was appalled!

A nice buffet dinner was served at the Legion Club after the beautiful wedding. Harvey did buy Pizza for the Bride's Table, so those who really wanted Pizza, got it!

Ex-husband was no longer with wife # 2, and already had someone in mind for wife # 3. Maryanne was very nice and we became friends. Randy and Kitty were no longer together, so we didn't have the mess of everyone hating everyone else, which made it a peaceful affair! Randy came with Daniel and Kirsten, with no girlfriend in sight.

I thought it strange that the newlyweds were going to wait a couple of weeks for the honeymoon, but nothing is ever normal in our family anyway.

We celebrated my birthday, which was exactly one week away, in Harvey and Lori's hotel room before they left for Chicago.

Exactly one week from the day after the wedding, Mr. & Mrs. Lewis and Bumper took me out to eat.

What a surprise when I walked in the room and there was Harvey and Lori, and about 40 friends! They had flown back from Chicago for my 50th birthday. It was a total surprise, and I'm still not sure I like surprises like that. Had I known, I would have worn something nicer. I would have put on my make-up more carefully and I would have had my hair done, I would have acted surprised in a more graceful way. What a wonderful party and family. They love me! Now I knew why the honeymoon was postponed. They had delayed it because of my big surprise birthday party!

BUMPER'S MIRACLE

Bumper and I had dinner at a friend's home and returned to our home about 6:oo in the evening. Bumper was feeling just fine. He walked into the house, put a leash on his dog, Cog, and took him outside. I was standing in the window when I saw him collapse in the driveway. I knew Bumper would not fall down unless he was in a lot of trouble, so I immediately called 911, and told them it was a definite heart attack and to get moving. By this time, they knew me well enough that directions to our house were not necessary, even though we lived eight miles out of Zimmerman, on a road used only by locals. I was hoping I was wrong about him needing help and could cancel the ambulance, but I knew better when I got to him. He was as gray as a navy ship of war, haze gray. I felt for a pulse, but there was none. Knowing no one could get near Bumper with Cog there, I picked him up and threw him in the house. I ran back to Bumper and started mouth-to-mouth resuscitation. I knew if I started giving CPR I could not stop, and one person can pass out doing it alone for any length of time. At that moment, a truck came by, and saw that Bumper was down on the ground. At first he thought Bumper was a drunk, until he saw what I was doing. He jumped out. His wife took off in the truck as he started CPR. In a few moments the truck came back. His wife had picked up a neighbor a few doors away, that unknown to me, were good at CPR. It was a miracle that the truck had come by at that time, and that he had left our neighbors house at that exact time! Everything that happened that day was a true miracle from God. You just do not have that many coincidences in a row! One of the men that did CPR on bumper wasn't sure he believed in a Higher Power, but after that day, his faith was restored.

They couldn't get a pulse, but if they hadn't done CPR, no one would ever have gotten one. "Mouth to mouth" helped save him too, so that he never went without oxygen for more than a few seconds. That is all it took for me to dial 911 and throw the Cog in the house.

The ambulance arrived and they continued CPR to no avail, until another big paramedic rig came from Princeton. They zapped Bumper many times with a defibrillator.

During all this time, I was very calm, which was another gift from God. I called Sonja when they were working on Bumper in the driveway, and thought I'd better let them know what was going on in case he didn't make it. I just told her that, in a while, they would be taking Bumper to Princeton Hospital, and then flying him to North Memorial Hospital in Minneapolis.

I will never know, to this day, what made me feel that I knew that. I told her to call the kids, two of whom lived in the city. She did call them and they were all there to meet us when we got to North Memorial. I was so calm that she didn't panic, and that started a chain reaction of keeping all of them calm. I told the helicopter crew of his wish not to be put on a Jarvic, and to make sure the hospital staff knew that.

During the time the paramedics were working on Bumper, I did not pray to bring him back. I prayed for God to do what was best for him. He would never want to be brought back to be a vegetable, or put on a Jarvick and still not make it. Never once did I scream that I wanted God to give him back. God doesn't always answer our prayers in the way we ask, but he does answer them, and I think sometimes He wants us to just leave it up to Him.

Some neighbors, who belonged to our church drove by, at the time they were working on Bumper, and immediately called the church, where a concert was going on. The minister stopped the concert, and prayers were said right there and then for him. This was long before they had gotten a pulse. Finally, Dan, a good friend, came up to me and said the best words I have ever heard, "They just got a pulse." Unconscious, they took him to Princeton Hospital, and loaded him in a helicopter for the trip to North Memorial Hospital in Minneapolis.

Dan's wife, Donna, said she would drive me down, because it was hard for her to believe I was not in a state of shock, which in truth I wasn't. I knew I could drive, but being "night blind", I thought she would feel better if I would let her drive. After a few minutes in the car, I realized we both had night blindness, but that was not on my list of things to worry about right then.

I tried to call Mother-in-Law before we left, but she was not home. I didn't want to leave a message like that on the answering machine, so I hung up, knowing it would be better to talk to her in person later.

Intensive care was touch and go because his already damaged heart was now even more damaged than before. His next adventure would be to have a heart transplant.

As soon as Bumper got out of intensive care, he called all the kids and told them that since he had died, and had been brought back to life, he now had two birthdays, and he wanted presents! Of course he got them! Even the ambulance crew sent him a bouquet of surgical gloves, blown up with helium.

Bev, a woman who fixed dinner that Sunday, wanted me to ask Bumper if he had seen a light in the tunnel. He had, with one of his previous surgeries, but this time, he told me that he had seen nothing. He asked me to dial Bev, and then took the phone. He said, "Bev, I saw the tunnel, and I saw the light. I headed down the tunnel, and there was this huge table spread with food. It looked good, and then they told me that you cooked it, so I got my ass right back down to earth." Does that sound like a man just out of intensive care? His ribs were hurting, but the doctor said it was a miracle that no ribs were broken, which almost always happens from

CPR.

When Bumper was about to leave the hospital, after two weeks, his heart started missing beats. Thank God we hadn't brought him home yet. He was put on a brand new drug that only cost $300.oo a month. Social Security disability doesn't pay for drugs. Our medical insurance had run out, so we had to find something soon. That expensive drug made his heart work better, but it was not the only drug he was taking.

From then on I was a nervous wreck, because after you have seen a loved one-drop over dead, you know it could happen again.

Bumper and I, (Mostly I) discussed the need for a transplant while he was still in the hospital. I thought he would welcome it, because it was his only chance to be well again. " If God wanted you, He has had lots of time to take you, so that must mean you will live through anything." He sort of listened! While he was in the hospital, I was thinking that I had more problems than I could handle, although Sonja was now healthy, Grandpa had just died and the bills were piling up. After a short time, I knew that I was thinking wrongly. I had to stop worrying about problems that could not be solved by me. If I continued to fret about everything, I would have no room for all the new troubles that would most certainly come. I know of no living person with out problems, unless they either lie, or are in a mental hospital where they have no idea what a problem is.

When Bumper got home from the hospital, he sat on the couch and cried, because he had thought he would never see home again. Cog and cat both sat right down with their daddy. From then on he would go to the doctor two times a week, so I would need another day off from the Barbershop. Oh well!

Sometimes I would feel, and I'm sure others with a sick person at home feel the same way, that I was completely tied down, and didn't feel I was living a life of my own. I would think that, but then, I would think how lucky I was to have Bumper. Some people have much worse problems; like living with a wife beater, drunk, or some other bad thing, but I don't have those problems. Yes, things could certainly be worse! I used to think I had problems when money was my only problem, but now, even though we are thousands of dollars in debt with medical bills, money problems seem very minor. When you have life and death situations, all other problems are small.

And yes I do believe in miracles!

IACCOA

In 1988 we decided we should get a new car. Our three- year-old car was almost paid for. We had two reasons to buy a new one. A heart patient didn't need a car that might not start. We needed a car with a warranty. Ours would expire in one year. The second reason, if Bumper were to die, I would own the car, because, the insurance we bought, stated that if either of us were to die the car would be paid for. If I could own a new car instead of the old one, that would make more sense. If he didn't die and the car had to be paid for, that would be even better.

We decided that waiting would not be a good idea, because Bumper was not doing well. At the Chrysler lot, I spotted the car I wanted. The car I needed! The most beautiful car in the world! A brand new Chrysler Lebaron sports model. RED!

After spotting my car, all others in the lot were hidden in fog. Bumper was trying to explain that it was a little expensive, but if you are going to spend a few thousand for a car, what is a few thousand more? If he died, I would have a beautiful car. If he lived we would just throw a few more bills in the trash and let the bill collectors have a field day trying to make us pay more medical bills with less money. Who cares? Bumper agreed with my way of thinking. He also adores me, so I got the car of my dreams. Our credit was good enough to go around the world, but we had no money! We drove my pride and joy home that day.

The next day, Bumper had a doctor's appointment. Even with the new car, there was no less stress getting him there. He was still mad that his lucky clothes had been trashed.

We got to the doctor feeling like we had come on a smooth cloud.
At least I did. Bumper had so much valium in his body, that he <u>was</u> on a cloud.

We got the news Bumper didn't want to hear. Dr. Azzam was sending him to the University Medical Center. He had made arrangements for them to do surgery to implant an AICD, which was a defibrillator inside his body. The AICD would shock his heart into starting if it stopped, or if the heart beat became erratic.
That surgery would be done in a couple of weeks, putting it at the very end of August. Bumper was scared of going to the University Hospital, because he knew that heart transplants were done there.

Having a defibrillator installed wasn't a transplant, so he figured that wouldn't be so bad.

On the way home, when we got onto the highway going north, our beautiful car broke down. QUIT! I eased it onto the shoulder and there we sat. The temperature had reached 104 degrees. That heat can do in a healthy person; say nothing about a heart patient. Our CB wasn't hooked up to our new car yet, so my nerves were starting to unravel. Bumper kept saying, "Stay calm." Of course I would stay calm. No problem! The car was heating up fast. I was so calm that I decided I'd better get out and start flagging cars down. I did that, and not one car stopped. I suppose they could see that a big man was sitting in the car. I can't blame them for not stopping.

My calm state of mind told me that I'd better get down on my knees and pray, in the hopes that a car with someone religious in it would stop and wonder why I was praying on the roadside. Bumper had been in the heat too long and my calmness was telling me that I was scared out of my wits!

Many, many cars went by, then a semi truck pulled over. If I could describe true relief in my lifetime, that semi truck stopping for us would be it. I explained our plight and he said, “Both of you hop in. I don’t have air-conditioning, but I will get you to the first place that does”. Those words sounded wonderful.

I didn’t realize how long and high a semi really was, until I tried to climb into it. Overweight and out of shape makes climbing into one of those a real challenge. Bumper then got in, and with the windows wide open for air, he took us down the road to the first place we saw, PERKINS! Thanking him with all our hearts, we rolled out and entered a world of coolness.

Having a cold drink, Bumper called the Chrysler Company and said, “come pick up the car, but pick us up in an air-conditioned car, because we are not going to ride in a hot tow truck”. They picked us up in a car, followed by a tow truck. At the Chrysler garage they gave us a nice loaner car to use.

The next morning, I wanted Lee Iaccoa to know about my beautiful car. I wrote a letter, but a letter of complaint wouldn’t get past his secretaries, so I wanted a letter that he would get personally. The copy of the letter was misplaced in all the stress, but I remember what I wrote.

Dear Mr. Iaccoa,

I bought a beautiful Red Chrysler Lebaron just two days ago. My dream car! The next morning, I took my husband to the doctor in Minneapolis in the new car. Things went fine until we headed for home. The new car broke down on highway 694, with temperatures of 104 degrees. My husband has a severe heart problem. That temperature isn’t good for a healthy person, so I think you would understand our situation! I tried to flag cars, but none would stop. I had my teeth in, a girdle on, so my looks couldn’t have been what prevented them from picking me up. They no doubt saw a brand new car and thought I was bluffing. I’ve seen a lot of cars stranded along the road, but none of them have been brand new Chryslers. That doesn’t look good for your company.

After trying everything, I got down on my knees and tore my nylons, to pray. A nice trucker was the only one to care. Do you know how hard it is to get a rotund body into a big semi? The nice man took us to an air-conditioned place where we could call Chrysler for help. They were very nice, came and picked us up and gave us a loaner. I have no complaints.

I'm not even complaining about my new car, I still love it. The only thing I am asking, is if this happens again, I want you to pay for my stay in a mental hospital, where I will most assuredly need to go.

The situation could have turned deadly with the heat, but God was protecting us, and we were OK, but I do not think God would pay for my stay in the loony bin!

I just want you to know what did happen to one of your new cars. If it happens again, would you come visit me in my new home that you will pay for?

Thank you!

The letter did get past the secretary, because I got a personal letter from him. He felt bad about the situation. He would check with the factory to make sure it wouldn't happen again and he appreciated the letter. I was hoping he would give me a free months payment or something, but at least my letter got to HIM!

Two days after that ordeal, Chrysler called to say the car was ready. The whole computer system had gone down.

Bumper told them to please deliver the car to us and drive the loaner back. He would feel better with them putting on those first miles instead of us. They did, and the car worked fine ever after.

AICD

At the end of August 1988, Bumper was scheduled at the University Hospital to have surgery to install the AICD, which was a defibrillator. Two women surgeons inserted it, with two paddles connected to his heart, which would shock him if the heart should fail.

After the three hour procedure, the two surgeons came out and said that he would have to come back to be evaluated for the heart transplant list. I was told that his heart was a mess, and that they would schedule an appointment for him before he left the hospital, which would be in a couple of days. If the other organs checked out O.K., he would be put on a waiting list very soon. I think they expected this news to be shocking to me, but they were not telling me a thing I didn't already know. My mixture of emotions was fear mixed with relief! At least he could maybe get a new heart. My biggest concern was that something would be wrong and they could not do a transplant. If that would happen, all hope would be lost, because that was his last chance for life. My other prayer was that the AICD would keep him alive until that time.

Bumper didn't fight the decision of the two doctors to get him in for transplant evaluation. He was starting to resign himself to the inevitable.

The day before I brought him home, the doctors had me notify the Sheriff's Department and the Ambulance Crew about the AICD, as it was new and unheard of by most people. I had a letter from the University Medical Department, stating that if they needed to pick him up, no radio transmitting could be used around the installed instrument. It could prevent it from working, or even stop it. I notified the Sheriff's office and then had to tell all my ambulance crew friends. Each one on the crew was hoping that he wouldn't have to be picked up, and if he did, that they wouldn't be the one on duty This was something very new, which none of them knew a thing about. I was told that if it went off once, he was breathing and would be OK. On the third jolt, I should call 911 immediately!

With great fear I took him home, wishing he was still safely in the hospital and could have an evaluation NOW! I thought it strange they didn't just keep him and give him the tests, but bureaucracy requires that it be done their way. My fear of being around Bumper was intense, because the worry of that machine doing a jump-start was a real thing. I was always concerned that something could happen, this time it seemed more real.

Bumper was happy to be back home with his Cog and cat, but deep down, he missed the security and safety he had felt in the hospital.

That evening, about eight hours after being home, he called to me from the den where he was resting and watching T.V. I heard the call and went to check on him. He said, "The machine zapped me once." True fear, close to panic is what I felt. It zapped him again; very apparent because his body jolted when it went off. "I'm dialing 911, stay calm, they'll be here in a minute." My fingers found those three numbers, but I was so scared, I don't even remember dialing. As I stayed with him his body kept jumping from the zaps that never stopped. If his heart was in bad shape already, I knew those zaps weren't helping any.

The sound of the siren was a relief. I did find out later that all the way out, Ray and two others were swearing under their breath the whole trip. They were concerned because they had no idea what to do with the new and unknown equipment.

A Sheriff's car arrived about the same time. They tried to call the University Hospital about the machine, but didn't get through to anyone that knew a darn thing about the AICD. The Sheriff's

Deputy and the ambulance crew were all women, and one of the crew said to Bumper, “I`ve always wanted to get you in the bedroom, but not like this.” That broke the ice a little bit. He was taken by ambulance three miles to a baseball field in Zimmerman. The floodlights were turned on, and a chopper landed right in the middle of the field.

The faces of the chopper crew were familiar to Bumper, because he had been with them before on a previous trip. His body was still jumping from the jolts, and the chopper crew didn’t know anything about the new equipment either. When the Sheriff's Deputy informed them they could not use a radio, they didn’t show the fear they must have felt. The Sheriff still had not been able to get a doctor that knew anything about the AICD on the phone, so the chopper crew would have to land on the roof of the University Hospital without radio contact. All the emergency room staff knew was that someone was coming in, but they knew nothing about the AICD either.

I couldn’t go along in the chopper, but tears were falling as I watched the big beautiful life saving bird ascend into the dark sky. “Oh God, be with Bumper and all of them,” I prayed through my sobs.

The journey was just beginning!

PART II

THE COCOON

EMERGENCY ROOM AND MAYO BUILDING

My neighbors took me to the University Hospital after the chopper had left. It had taken the chopper around 14 minutes. It took us almost an hour.

Bumper had been put into a small curtained room, still jumping from the jolts. I had a screaming fit that nothing had been done for him yet. His body had already jolted well over 30 times. How much could the poor heart stand?

Even in his present disastrous condition, Bumper was worried about me taking all of the stress, and asked the ER Doctor if I could have a Valium. I didn't get one.

I hadn't called any of the family yet, because I was far too distraught to deal with anything at the moment. A doctor came in and picked up a certain kind of magnet that was about ten feet away from Bumper, and turned the AICD off! Not many people had been on the AICD. Bumper was the seventeenth person to have been on an AICD at the University Hospital. I guess you could call him a "Pioneer."

Because they may have to take him to Intensive Care, they wanted me to go home for a while. The wonderful neighbors that had brought me to the hospital were my lifesavers that night. They took me home. I needed them, and they were there.

In the morning, Mother-in-Law and all the kids learned where Bumper was and came down later that day.

When I came back, his new home was ICU, but the main ICU in the new hospital was full, so he was in a temporary one in the old Mayo Building connected to the main hospital.

It was a large drab colored room with eight beds, which were no more than two feet apart. The care he was getting was very good. Through all of the agony and fear Bumper was feeling, his smile was the brightest thing my day had seen. He never seemed to be in a down mood.

Across from Bumper was a very large young man, about 18 or 19 years old. That poor man needed a new heart, kidney, and maybe even more organs. Bumper, in his miserable condition, was as strong as an ox compared to that young man.

The Transplant Coordinator, a very nice woman named Sophia, came to Bumper's bedside, and told him that as soon as a bed opened in the ICU of the new hospital, those in the room would be moved there as soon as possible. She also gave him the news that he wouldn't be leaving the hospital without a new heart. It was then that we knew he was there for the duration.

Bumper just looked at her and said, "Cal Stoll got a heart transplant, didn't he?" She said, "Yes, would you like to meet him?" "I would", said Bumper.

Cal Stoll used to coach Gopher Football (the University of Minnesota's Big 10 Team), and Bumper had always liked him. He claimed to be the last WINNING coach of the Gophers. Bumper was hoping that he would come, but he didn't know if Cal would have the time.

About three hours later, Bumper had a guest. It was Cal Stoll! I had never met Cal before, but the pep talk he was giving Bumper sure impressed me. He was the best person Bumper could have met.

Not only did he lift Bumper's spirits up, he took me with him. I was feeling better than I had since Bumper's arrival at the hospital.

When Cal left, the Transplant Coordinator came back and told Bumper that they would be doing tests to see if he was eligible for a transplant. All Bumper said to her was, "If Cal could do it, so can I!" Bumper was truly a rock and I was proud of him.

Coming in the next morning, I discovered that Bumper and the boy in the bed across from him had become fast friends. He had given Bumper a little bear that said "Get Well". I could see that Bumper thought that young man was pretty special, and what was left of his heart was going out to him.

Bumper told me that the young man needed a portable radio with earphones, and wanted me to bring one for him the next day. With all his own problems, Bumper was more concerned about someone else. This didn't surprise me!

A football game was coming up, and there were no TV's in the temporary ICU ward, but somehow some TV's were brought in. Maybe Cal had something to do with that. It sure brightened the lives of the guys' in that room.

Bumper spent over a week in that room, and I would cry all the way as I drove home. Sometimes, crying would make it hard to drive through downtown Minneapolis, but I was getting good at driving and crying at the same time. I knew I would look silly if a cop stopped me, but I couldn't help it.

Each day on the way home, I would stop by our friends, Mertin and Inga Illiff's house, and they would always have supper ready, which I didn't want them to do. I wanted to be out of the city before it turned dark, so I always came there about the same time. I would cry some more, as I just had to stop there and vent my feelings, and I was always welcome.

I kept the Barbershop open, although Melvin and Willie were not there anymore. I think Willie needed to make real money now that he was a Master Barber, and I knew he was doing the right thing. I kept the shop open in the mornings only, because I wanted to be with Bumper. My life was in a mess, and I felt as though I was slowly being sucked down a big drain, without being able to pull myself up. I was feeling sorry for me, and that was not a good thing to do, because Bumper was the one who was sick.

The whole time he was in the dormitory, he was being evaluated medically. My emotions were flying during that time. I was afraid that maybe he couldn't get a transplant, then what? Death. I was afraid they would say he could have one and would put him on the list, where maybe he would get a heart, maybe not. If he did, he would get well, if he didn't? Death. Bumper must have had the same emotions, but we just couldn't discuss them.

We finally were told he was a candidate, and was on the list. Wonderful! Should I laugh or cry? The fear then shifted to the thought that maybe a heart wouldn't become available in time for him.

Everyone wanted money from me, and I didn't have any. Being in a life/death situation is hard enough for anyone, but I have to believe that it is made harder when the bills are piling up. I can't get my loved one well. I couldn't pay my bills, and I didn't know where to go from there. The merry-go-round was starting and it kept speeding up, making it impossible for me to jump off.

THE MERRY-GO-ROUND STARTS TURNING

I thought it would be nice to contact Bumper's brother who lived in California. It was not easy, because he was the only person I knew that used a pay phone on the pier for his personal phone. It was a somewhat happy occasion when he finally called Mother-in-Law collect from his private phone on the pier in San Diego.

David (the brother) decided that he would come home and stay until a heart came for Bumper. That was good news and I knew it would make Bumper happy.

Our family is not always one that would be considered normal, so David, the Vietnam Vet, fit right in. Leslee (Bumper's sister) also came back from Michigan for a few days, so a family re-union took place right there in the ICU.

When the new hospital had openings in that ward, many patients were transferred into the new ICU. Bumper's young friend was not among them, and we never heard any more about him. I was pretty certain he was not with us anymore.

Trying to keep the barbershop open was getting to be impossible, because I was often called from the hospital and told to come down, as he wasn't doing well.

One morning, I was called at the shop to come to the ICU. My poor customer had the fastest haircut in the world! I raced to the University Hospital in my new car, hoping a cop would escort me, but I didn't see one.

When I got there, Bumper wasn't in the room. I asked at the desk, and some nurse's aide or scrubwoman or someone, told me that a Peterson had just died, and she thought it was him. I went into a state of shock and called Pastor Tom, who was living in St. Paul at the time.

In the meantime, it was discovered that Bumper had been moved to a different room with more windows. When Pastor Tom got there, he went to see the head administrator of the hospital, and all hell broke loose. I was paged, and got an apology from the person in charge of the hospital, but that didn't cure the mental state I was in. I don't know what happened to that woman, but for some reason I didn't see her behind the desk anymore.

I was still driving through traffic crying each night, and stopping at Mert and Inga's for supper, which I usually had trouble keeping down, because my nerves were badly damaged by this time.

The merry-go-round was starting to spin; I was stuck on it, and couldn't get off. I had no idea which way to turn. How could I keep the shop open? How could I survive without an income? I could not answer any of these questions, and my mind and body were a mess. I wasn't sleeping. Fat was coming off my body. I looked thin but I felt awful.

I had to do something, or the merry-go-round would go into a tailspin and I could be stuck in space forever.

I made the decision that I would move into the city to be close to Bumper. It wasn't much, but it was a start. After that one decision was made, I felt much better, and the merry-go-round slowed down a bit. I started to think straight.

I told my friends that I was going to move to Minneapolis, and they all said, "How can you make it financially?" How the hell did I know? I just knew that I was going to do it! Once I stopped letting the merry-go-round run me, the choice I had made was a good one, because I felt a little in control and had a plan. I HAD to have a plan to survive this mess, and I was going to survive!

APARTMENT SEARCH

I closed up the shop, not knowing how long I would be gone. Jednecks, the owners, said they wouldn't charge me any rent, that I should just keep everything as it was until spring. We would know then what our future plans would be. Not many landlords would do that, but they were special, caring people. That wonderful news took a big chunk out of all the problems I was having. To implement my plan, I would visit Bumper each morning, and then head out to find a nice apartment. I needed one that would take a dog and a cat, was cheap, with no lease requirement, and in a good area. Finding a one legged high hurdler would have been an easier task.

I began my search by looking at apartments near the University. Everyplace that I looked at was noisy, run down, took no pets, and had a lease. So far, all the prices had been too high. I was batting 0! I moved my search to south Minneapolis, and the pickings were even slimmer. Only the slums were in my price range. I was not interested. Also, they wouldn't take two pets and all required a lease.

Knowing Bumper would have to stay in the city for three months following the transplant, I wanted something that was nice enough for him to call home after the heart transplant. I kind of wanted something in an area where I wouldn't have to be afraid to take out the garbage.

I had wasted one whole week looking for the impossible. When Jon learned of the trouble I was having locating a place, he said, "I'll take you to Apartment Search!" I hadn't heard of it. We went to the Apartment Search office, and I told the guy what I needed, knowing it was an almost impossible task. When the man showed us lots of options on a TV screen, I couldn't believe it!

We spotted a very nice apartment in Edina that had everything: 2 pools (Indoor and outdoor), hot tub, tennis courts, racquet ball, good movies one night a week, underground parking, and they allowed pets! The price was no more than the crumby ones I had been looking at near the University with no parking. Edina is an upscale suburb, so that sounded like Heaven to me!

Jon and I went to see the place, and it was nicer than our little home in Zimmerman. I did not have all those wonderful things!

They had exceptions on leases for emergency situations, so no lease was needed. Within minutes of seeing that beautiful place just off France Avenue, I had a place to call home.

Getting the apartment seemed to take a whole load off my shoulders, because now I knew what I was doing, and where I would be. Money was a problem. I knew we couldn't live forever on what we had in the bank, but I would use what we had and worry about the rest later. God, I felt good!

Getting ready to move would keep my body and mind busy, so the merry-go-round was slowing down, but still going around.

Bumper was happy that I would be living in the City, near him.

I would need to take furniture from our house for the unfurnished apartment, dishes and other things that I would need. It didn't take me long to get ready. I would be able to move in a few days, when David could get a hold of his cousin who had a much needed pick-up truck.

My fear and nervousness were still very much within me, but I could at least clear a small part for the excitement of moving closer to Bumper.

MOVING DAY

In describing my feelings about moving, I would have to say 'Bittersweet'. I could add to that 'being in limbo'. I was happy to know finally, what I was doing, right or wrong! Being near Bumper made moving a happy thought. Moving away from the place we had lived for so long, and raised the kids, was sad. The possibility that Bumper might never come back to this house was tearing me apart and I was crying. Living with no income was terrifying. Not knowing what was going to happen was putting me back on the merry-go-round that I was trying so hard to get off. Trying to realize that God works in mysterious ways seemed hard to believe. Some of my friends quoted that old saying, "sometimes things have to get worse to get better." They had been worse long enough!

I had to put Bandit, the cat, in a cage that he hated, so that when David came to move things out, Bandit wouldn't disappear. Cog was not one bit happy about the chaos, but he was not happy about Daddy being gone anyway, so I guess he was normal.

David and two cousins came with pickup trucks, and loaded everything up. David knew everything about moving, and that made me happy knowing that things would get there in good shape.

David and Steve were each driving a pickup, and Scott was driving my car. Cat was very unhappy in his cage. I had had to cover it, because he was terrified of riding in the car. He was howling and carrying on. I was hoping that he wouldn't die of a heart attack on the way. Cog was next to the cage in the back seat, growling each time I turned around to check on the two animals. Cog was not a happy camper. He was downright mad about all the nonsense and wanted to go home.

Before we got to Highway 494, one of my lamps fell off of David's truck, so he had to stop and retrieve it from the ditch. I could see it was a little dented but that was not on my list of things to worry about. I was glad that my sister had bought the new furniture, because if we were moving with the old stuff, we would have looked like Jed Clampett from the Beverly Hillbillies.

Things were going smoothly and I was beginning to know cousin Scott a bit better. We were on busy 494 when both of us saw underwear floating in front of us. As I sat in silence and watched all my clothes blowing away, Scott said, "Are those yours?" Of course they were mine. You could see them all billowing out of the dresser that David had said would be fine without the drawers being tied shut! "Should we stop and pick them up?" Scott said. "Oh absolutely! I will just run my ass out on the busy freeway, halt the cars, and start picking up my undies. Are you nuts?" I shouted. If I was stupid enough to do that, the Cog could have gotten out of the car. I would have had to chase that little devil, and maybe he would have been run over. That would have saved me a lot of trouble with the little beast, but Bumper would kill me when he got well. We didn't want to get in front of David and start honking, because my undies were gone anyway, and how could I chase them in the middle of traffic?

Getting to the apartment, the guys set everything up in the house, and left. I was alone with boxes and two not so happy animals. They didn't like the new place at all.

As I was unpacking dishes, Cog crapped all over the new white carpet. Lhasas have glands that must be cleaned out every so often, and being on the merry-go-round, I hadn't thought about that. Now what? In a strange place, not familiar with the area, I needed to locate a veterinarian on a Sunday night. My fingers "did the walking through the yellow pages," and I found a twenty-four hour veterinarian not far away, so I took the beast to him. I was used to him biting, so that didn't bother me anymore. The vet cleaned him out, so then all I had to worry about at the moment was getting doggy-do off the white carpet, and I had brought no cleaning supplies with me. A Target store was nearby, so I got some stuff to clean the carpet, and spent the next several hours on the floor.

I discovered that I had brought everything I didn't need, except for the furniture. I had no spoons, no bowls, no toilet paper, no underwear and very little money. I did have pictures for the wall and all that stuff. When a person moves under such "life and death conditions," they do strange things.

The carpet was finally cleaned, linens put on the bed, so I went to bed in my new surroundings. Cog had nothing to guard without Bumper, so I got into my own bed, a little scared of being in the new place in a big city. I was also scared that the merry-go-round would start up again.

HOSPITAL DAYS

Every morning I would get up and go to the hospital. Every morning a psychiatrist would go into Bumper's room and hypnotize him. The AICD was still in his body, but not in use because it was defective, and that is why it had gone off so many times. They had to keep him calm so his heart wouldn't stop, so that was the reason for the psychiatrist's visit. I was never in the room when he was hypnotized, and Bumper doesn't believe he was, but I know he was. They could not have Valium in his system if a heart were to become available, so hypnosis was the next best thing.

Bumper was like a ping-pong ball going between fourth floor Intensive Care, and the sixth floor Heart Ward. He would go into ventricular attack (v tac), an erratic heartbeat, or his heart would stop and down he would go to fourth floor. When he was stable, up he would go to sixth. Ping-pong! I would come any given day, and have no idea which floor he would be on.

A priest stopped to see Bumper daily. He was the sweetest guy, but we were not Catholics, I didn't know it at the time, but I later heard that he was part of an evaluation team to see if we were both mentally stable enough to deal with a new heart, and if Bumper's outlook on life was good. Bumper had the best disposition and outlook of anyone I had ever seen! It's a good thing the priest didn't see me outside the hospital.

When any spouse has to go in day after day to see someone, they will always be cheerful and tell them everything is going well. Lying each day gets very hard, but I believe most spouses do it. I should have gotten an academy award for acting so calm and happy. The only way to describe how I really felt is "LIKE SHIT!" That would be an honest description, tacky, as it may seem. I wasn't eating much because my stomach was nervous. I wasn't sleeping well because the rest of me was nervous. I was scared for Bumper, scared for me, worried about money, frantic that a heart may not come, but looking terrific because I was losing a lot of weight. My clothes no longer fit so I had to find some smaller ones, which under other circumstances would have been wonderful.

When Mother-in-Law and David were there each day, I would spend time finding my way around the huge hospital. I knew every tunnel going to every building connected to the hospital. I could have given tours, I was that good. If people looked as though they were lost, I would ask what they were looking for, and I would get them there.

One of Bumper's doctors, Dr. Wang, was also Sonja's doctor, so it was nice to have two in the family with the same cardiologist. Bumper always laid in bed with a wet washcloth on his head, and Dr. Wang would ask him "Why do you have that rag on your head?" Bumper would just smile and say nothing. Maybe the reason came from the hypnotist because it would help him stay calm? We never did know why.

Dental work should be done before transplant, because cavities could cause infection, which can be serious for a transplant patient. Bumper needed dental work done, but he was terrified of dentists. He was as afraid of them as he had been of Dr. Azzam before he came to the University of Minnesota Hospital. He no longer had to fear the statement "You need a transplant". The dentist was another story.

One day they wheeled his bed over to the dental school, which was connected to the hospital by tunnels. On the way, his heart stopped and they had to use resuscitation paddles to get it going. That scared the staff so much that it was decided the dental work would have to wait until he had a new heart. They did away with taking patients to the dental school, deciding it was too risky to be that far away from all the special equipment and trained help. He did change something! Bumper was no longer afraid of having a transplant, and knew he would rather have a transplant than go to the dentist. The doctors got a charge out of that.

Every time I was driving the car, I played a sick game. I know that everyone who has someone waiting for an organ may do the same thing. I would be so frustrated that the heart was taking so long to come, that I would size up people walking in front of the car. Were they the same size? I wondered what blood type they had? Then I figured that their hearts might not be a match for Bumper's heart, so I didn't run them over after careful thought. You would have had to be much crazier than me to really do it.

The merry-go-round wasn't turning anymore. I felt that I was in an airplane, with God as the pilot, and I could do nothing but go along on the trip. Barf bags were included, so I could throw up when needed.

THE APARTMENT

Our daughter, Heidi, was working at Canterbury Downs, a racetrack just south of Minneapolis. She had been staying with a friend and was looking for an apartment, so she decided that it was the perfect time for her to move in with mother. She was between boyfriends, so I was happy about her living with me. A guy with three kids just wasn't my idea of bliss for my lovable daughter who was having trouble with choosing suitable men.

We sat in the hot tub most evenings and I was starting to relax to some degree, now that God was the pilot of my trip. I was no longer the only one that Cog didn't like in the house. Heidi was my competition. I think he may have hated her more than me! Bandit was happy to have Heidi around again, but then, Bandit had brains, and had known her since he was a kitten. I was starting to like the place, because it didn't have all the junk that I had accumulated at home. I learned it was possible to keep an uncluttered place clean.

Heidi was a blessing to me at the time. She said that she would stay until Bumper's heart came and the transplant had been done, and then move into a place with some friends, and maybe get a new boyfriend. With all the problems that I was having, her mentioning a new boyfriend didn't help my relaxation efforts. What would she come up with next?

Bumper had now been in the hospital for about two months. After being by his side all day, it was nice to have a 20 minute drive to a clean place with a pool, compared to an hour drive through traffic, to a cabin in the woods, with none of the luxuries that I had quickly learned to love. My life was put on hold, or should I say was still in limbo, but I was surviving and feeling a little better than before. I was still losing weight and looking good. I could have passed for having a normal life.

INSURANCE

Bumper came into the hospital the very first week of September. The last week of October, the insurance company said he had to leave the hospital because they were doing nothing for him. He couldn't stay in the hospital to wait for an organ unless he needed to be hooked up to machines, which Bumper didn't. His only problem was that his heart stopped quite often, which would make him dead, but that wasn't a serious enough illness for the insurance company to allow him to stay in the hospital.

David and I had a meeting with the hospital administrators, and the doctors and nurses agreed that Bumper should not go out into the general population, because his chances for survival would be 0. The hospital tried to fight with the insurance company, but they were losing the battle.

I said, "under no circumstances will I take him home. I will not be here to get him." David said that he would not take Bumper home to our apartment because he knew he had no business leaving the hospital.

The doctors were mad about the decision that he must leave. They told us that if it actually happened, we should take him out, drive around the block and bring him back in. That way it would be a new account and they could re-admit him.

That was nice of the doctors, but what if his heart stopped when walked out of the front door? He would not be a patient. He would be dead. If not, he'd wait for an ambulance to come to the front door to get him. No way would I let that happen. David and I could both be nasty and mean, and we were good at it. Because of our efforts, the hospital agreed that he could stay one more week, but on Tuesday November 7th, we would have to take him home.

That made us all angry, but what the heck? We would not show up and would they put him in a cab with no money? I doubted that!

Bumper was nervous about that awful decision, and being nervous was not good for him. David and I promised we would not bring him home. Knowing us, he knew we meant it!

That was a week full of fear and stress. I still had the co-pilot and my barf bags for my plane, so I tried not to get too upset. I BELIEVED!

D-DAY

Monday, November 6th, was just a regular uneventful day in hospital ward 6C. We spent most of the day there, because the uncertainty of the next day made us all a little anxious. Being the hospital ping-pong ball, we knew that the possibility of Bumper going back to 4C was great. Thinking about November 7th and being thrown out of the hospital was stressful for him, but if he could get back to ICU they couldn't release him. It's awful to want your loved one to go back to the ICU. That is a scary place, but under the circumstances we were facing, it would be a welcome and safe haven. At least being there could buy him a few more days, and then maybe we could have another meeting with the hospital management, and those few days might bring in a heart for his transplant.

Leaving the hospital that day, I had my normal cry while driving home. I was worried about Bumper, but I was also concerned about his damn dog. Cog was in some sort of dog depression and had stopped eating. I got him to eat enough to sustain him, but he wasn't his normal ugly, mean, little self. I knew the reason was because Daddy had been gone too long. Bandit, on the other hand, was content to get affection and love just from me.

I had talked to Bumper on the phone before getting ready for bed, and he seemed quite relaxed. That un-nerved me, because he didn't sound like a candidate for 4C, which is Intensive Care. At 10:00 that night, about a half hour after I had talked to him, Mother-in-Law called frantically saying that she was talking on the phone to Bumper, and she heard someone come in the room and say something about a heart. She said Bumper dropped the phone and that is all she heard.

I called the desk in 6C and asked what was happening with Bumper. The wonderful words "We think we may have a heart for him" was all I needed to hear.

I called Mother-in-Law, and she said that David would be taking us and he would be by to pick me up shortly. In that short time, I called all four of the kids, and they would all be on the way. Heidi had just moved into a place with some friends, so she would be coming from River Falls, Wisconsin.

I called Pastor Tom, leaving a message with his son that Bumper was going to get a heart.

I called Mertin and Inga, because they wanted to know no matter what time it was. That collect call was the best birthday present Mertin had received. He had only about an hour and a half left of his birthday.

Everyone seemed to hit 6C about the same time, meaning some had to have driven a little faster than others. Pastor Tom was there, so his son Steve had given him the message immediately. Bumper had a whole entourage at the lounge area at the end of the hall. I already knew that almost everyone receiving an organ has an entourage as big, or bigger, so we were not the only ones to look like a head of state was in there.

They told us where the heart was coming from, at least what area, but I understand that they no longer do that. We knew it was coming from Denver, and that doctors had flown out to remove the heart from the donor, and bring it back to Minneapolis. Now I had something to worry about! I worried that the plane would crash! That was my only problem at the minute. The kids were wishing Bumper's hypnotist would come by to take care of me, but no luck!

One at a time, we got to see Bumper for only a minute, because the staff was taking blood and getting him ready. They were doing everything possible to keep him calm, and they didn't want us close to him.

Everyone was carrying on some type of conversation except me. I was deep in thought thinking about the plane crash that would maybe happen soon, and I was trying to ask God to keep it from crashing. My mind was going!

They wheeled him down to the Operating Room, and we said goodbye to him. A few minutes later, we were told the plane was on the ground, and the heart would be here in a few minutes. They were bringing it by helicopter to the hospital. What did I do then? I worried about the helicopter crashing. My family was worried about me.

As we were sitting in the lounge, Pastor Tom informed me that the helicopter had landed on the roof. I did such a personality transformation that I was a good candidate for the mental illness of dual personality.

I shed maybe 100 pounds of stress, and had nothing more to worry about. Ignorance, along with being naïve, is bliss, so the thought didn't cross any of our minds that something could go wrong during surgery. We decided we would go home, maybe get some sleep, and come back refreshed and worry free the next day.

We left the hospital very early in the morning of November 7th, Jon and Merri's first wedding anniversary. He was getting the heart in time for my birthday. November 7th was a very important day.

I went back to the apartment, but I didn't sleep. I had promised so many friends that I would call them the minute Bumper got his heart. I did that, in fact calling them collect, telling them he was getting his heart, and would be fine and healthy again. Not one of them got mad at me for the late hour, or the collect call.

4-D

I went to see Bumper the next day. He was still hooked up to the heart lung machine, but awake. It was a surprise to see the beautiful color in his face. He had been ashen for so many years. It was also a surprise to see he had gained about 20 pounds in the few hours since I saw him last. He seemed agitated but couldn't speak with the big tube going down his throat. He was able to write to some degree, and the word he wrote was 'fat'. His nurse explained that they had filled him with fluid during transplant, but we should not worry; it would come off very shortly.

All the other times he had been in the ICU, he was in 4C, and had the same primary care nurse, Ann, whom everyone adored. This time, being in 4D, the ward where you go after surgery, he was without Ann, and the security of her excellent care. The care was just as good in 4D, but unfamiliar to him.

Everyone had to put on scrubs to go into his room after transplant. Head, feet, hands, all had to be covered. They stuck with the rules that he could have two visitors at a time, ten minutes out of each hour and family members only. The rules have changed since then, scrubs are no longer necessary, and visiting rules are more liberal. I had a lot of time to spend exploring the hospital that I already knew so well.

Between Mother-in-Law, the kids, David and me, ten minutes of each hour were taken up.

He had also acquired a couple of new relatives, Mr. and Mrs. Lewis, who became a brother and sister in law that the nurses didn't know weren't his legally.

As soon as he got off the heart lung machine, all the water weight disappeared and he looked good. It felt good to get off that big machine too. A couple of days and he was out of ICU, back on 6C.

Going to the hospital each day become a joy, and I no longer cried all the way home. I was busy getting things ready for his coming home to the new place, which would be about Thanksgiving time.

We were both entering into a new world of Bumper being healthy and feeling good, a world that had become lost to us. I had forgotten what it felt like for me to feel good, but I did. Both Bumper and Sonja were now well, and so much fear and stress was lifted off my shoulders.

How did it happen that the heart came on the day he was supposed to be released? I don't even wonder because I think I already know!

THANKSGIVING DAY 1988

The best Thanksgiving we have ever had was the day Bumper was released from the hospital. I was filled with excitement, but seeing Bumper's face when he came through the door of our new home, I knew my excitement level hadn't reached its peak until that moment.

The beautiful Christmas tree and neat uncluttered place caught his misty eyes. More important than that, two very happy animals were standing inside the door waiting for him. His wet eyes turned to sparkle, and then full tears. Cog and Cat had their Daddy home, and those three were a picture of happiness that could never be captured.

Bumper didn't bother to look at the rest of the new home until all three had given each other the loving hugs they so deserved. True happiness, laughter, tears, relaxation, love, contentment and thankfulness were how I would have described my feelings.

The kids were together for Thanksgiving, but we wouldn't have joined them even if Bumper hadn't just gotten out of the hospital. Little children, even if they are not sick can spread germs, so with our grandchildren, Daniel and Kirsten, being so tiny, we would not have taken a chance by being near any children quite yet.

Mother-in-Law was at David's, so everyone had a wonderful Thanksgiving, but ours was the best, spending the day alone in our new place, with our pets.

Within an hour after his Daddy's homecoming, Cog didn't want me around any more, but the arrogant little mutt was now stuck with me too. Cat was very friendly toward me, because I hadn't left him for all that time, and had cared for him and loved him in Daddy's absence.

SECOND CHANCE FOR LIFE

Bumper's recovery days were, I think, the best days of our lives. He was healthy and we could do things together. We spent much of our time getting to know Minneapolis and St. Paul.

Most of all, we spent our time with Second Chance for Life, which is a support group for Heart Transplants run by Heart Transplants and their spouses. They all became our extended family, and we still love every one of them.

The group was started before we came into it, but it was small. Cal Stoll who was the University of Minnesota football coach from 1972 through 1978 was the head of Second Chance. He gave credit for its beginning to three other guys. They may have helped with the idea, but Cal Stoll was Second Chance for Life. Cal received a heart in July of 1987. He would get up every morning and thank God for his Donor, and kiss his wife June and tell her that he loved her. He taught all of us that we should do the same. He said "If you don't feel good, don't whine about it if it's something far away from the heart. Just live with it!" He tried to be the tough guy, but he was the sweetest, most gentle pussycat in the world.

Second Chance is the most elite group in the world. You cannot buy your way in. It must be earned through having a heart transplant, or being on the waiting list. It started out small, but twelve years later, it has about 600 pre and post thoracic transplants, because it was also opened to those in need of lungs.

Cal had the name, so he knew how to get funding. Second Chance helps anyone that is in need of money, housing, or friendship. Sick people come from all over the world and need a place to stay. At one time, very little was available in affordable housing, and if people couldn't make it, Second Chance helped them. Second Chance still does help, although the hospital has some apartment buildings now, but you still need money to pay for them.

If there is a need for food or medicine, Second Chance will help. Many people waiting for either a heart or lung, have to move here sick, and with no job. We all know what they are going through, so we give them support.

Each July, we have a big re-union for transplant recipients and those waiting for a heart or lung. It is the highlight of the year. Those living in the Minneapolis area have it best, because we have gotten to know most of them coming through the system.

If they cannot afford the gas to come to the reunion, Second Chance sends them gas money. If they can't afford a hotel, Second Chance is there. Cal didn't want anyone to miss this event because they couldn't afford it.

All hospitals have support groups, but none of them have the financing and ability to help those in need like Second Chance does. We have friends all over the United States in this group and they are true friends. Bumper and I are proud to be a part of this select and elite group, but the qualifications for membership were, and still are, very hard. You earn your way in!

Cal, lovingly called by all 'The Coach', was a true mentor and kept us from feeling sorry for ourselves. He would be hard as nails on someone who would let that happen. He taught us to realize EVERYDAY IS CHRISTMAS, and it is!

Cal died August 25,2000. All of us at Second Chance for life have lost our best friend.

HOMEWARD BOUND

It was difficult, although wonderful, having Bumper able to do things. However, his first venture out alone became a nightmare for me. We lived only a few blocks from a Target store, and he wanted to go there. It was hard to let him go off on his own when he had needed me with him for so long. He hadn't even driven by himself for months. Going to Target would only take a short while, so off he went. It was almost like seeing a child off to school for the first day without me. I didn't get too concerned until an hour later. By one and a half hours I was a total basket case. It was broad daylight. He was a grown man. Why was I getting so hyper? This was a new situation for me and I wasn't handling it well. When Bumper had been gone two hours, I called the Edina Police to see if he had been in an accident. They didn't know of any. I then called Fairview Southdale hospital to see if he was admitted. "NO." Next, I called the University Hospital to see if he had been admitted there, since that hospital was on the medical alert tag, which he wore around his neck. No, they hadn't heard from him. I was pacing the floor and going absolutely bananas when the door opened and in sauntered my dear Bumper. At first, I was worried. When I saw he wasn't hurt I was mad, but now, I was FURIOUS! Bumper is so long winded that he can talk to friends or strangers for hours, and that was what he had done. He hadn't seen me that mad for a long, long time, and promised to keep closer tabs on the time when he went out. After my rage, I couldn't help but laugh, because it was ridiculous for me to get so worried. He had been sick for so long, I just didn't know how to react to him being well enough to be out on his own.

We were planning to move back home on March 1st, but they spotted something on his lung, so we decided to stay until his next x-ray, to see if it was still there. We felt secure in our little cocoon and were not in a big hurry to leave the place where we were so happy.

One night, the first part of April, we decided to drive along the Mississippi river in downtown St. Paul. We took a road where the riverboats were docked and headed into the woods. Being adventurous, we had to see where it would lead us. It was a gravel road, so continuing on, it turned a little muddy. Going further into the dark unknown river swamp, the road turned into a path. The river was suddenly on both sides of us, and it was impossible to turn around. The night was as black as coal. Our imaginations were running wild, with no street lights to guide us. The tree-lined path was turning into a nightmare. The next thing we thought we would see was a swamp monster dragging a bloody, lifeless body. Bumper was beginning to get goosebumps. We were close to downtown, but yet, in pure wilderness. If we were to get stuck, we would sit there for a long, long time, or have to walk back a great distance. We didn't know what was ahead. We both wished that we had a gun, and that Bumper had brought his anti-rejection drug, plus all his other medicines, in case we were stranded there all night. I imagined a perfect murder, or at least the dumping of bodies. There couldn't have been a better place for that. I hoped we wouldn't spot one! I knew I was scared, but I tried to act brave so Bumper wouldn't be scared. He was trying to act bravely so that I wouldn't be scared. We both did a rotten job of acting. The road seemed to go on forever. What a relief it was when finally we spotted a building ahead of us. It was a yacht club or something, which was closed for the season. At least civilization couldn't be far. Going past the club, we spotted the highway up ahead. Our nightmare was over and we were still alive and well. We never did regret that mystery trip down by the river. Maybe we needed the excitement!

After another chest x-ray a few weeks later, the spot on his lung was gone, so we could leave for home. By now, I loved the area and didn't want to go home, but we packed up and asked David, the great mover, to come with the pickups again.

Everything was out of the house. Cog was in the car, but Bandit, the cat, was nowhere to be found. The 17-year old cat had become my love, and I was in tears looking for him. David said to just leave him; he had probably gotten outside and was lost. No way! I said that I would sit forever until I found him. He had become scared when the moving started, and I had been so careful, that I didn't see how he could have run out. I started going through everything in the whole place, and finally found him up in a closed kitchen cupboard. I think he was as happy to see me, as I was to see him. He survived well in his covered cage for the trip home.

It was nice to be back to our home in the woods, but we should have been happier. It was then that I knew we would have to make some important decisions, because I felt this was not where I wanted to be at this time in my life. What a mixture of feelings. Happy to be home, but I already missed the excitement of the city, and my friends in Second Chance for Life.

PART III

THE BUTTERFLY

BACK HOME

On April 20, 1989 Jon and Merri had their first baby, a little girl that they named Kayla Marie. While in the hospital, the doctors discovered that Merri was diabetic. Kayla suffered from sleep apnea. She had to wear a monitor, because she could die in her sleep if there was no alarm to wake her. I was scared to death to take care of her, so I wasn't much help. Bumper was so recently out of transplant that taking care of a baby was not a good idea because little babies and children carry germs. We saw her, but didn't really help with her care, because we didn't live that close to them. Three grandchildren. I guess we were getting old!

I reopened the Barber Shop, but business wasn't good, because most of my customers had gone elsewhere. The town of Zimmerman is small, but the surrounding area is big. I knew I would have to do a lot of advertising, and it would still take a long time to get my customers back. I didn't have a lot of money for advertising, and I didn't know if I wanted to stay, so I just bided time until we figured out where we wanted to spend the rest of our lives. I was quite sure it wasn't in Zimmerman.

Mr. and Mrs. Lewis were living in Willmar, Minnesota. We would spend some weekends with them, and they would spend some weekends at our place. One Saturday night in May, as we were playing cards, and the men were pouting because Mrs. Lewis and I were winning, a large truck pulled into the driveway. It was larger than a pickup truck and something of a rattletrap. I wondered who would come to visit us in that thing. A few minutes later, I saw my sweet little Heidi coming toward the house with the latest love of her life that she had been bragging about. He looked like a bear that had just come out of the mountains after a long winter. The beard was short, but he looked unkempt. A closer look at Heidi and she looked the same way but without a beard. The minute the two of them entered the house; we knew Heidi was serious about this mountain man when she said he was a trapper. The smell gave both of them away. He earned a living by picking up hides and pelts from all over the north country that he bought for fur companies that made coats out of them. Heidi was beaming when she introduced us to her true love, the one she was sure she would marry. She had met Rob in college at River Falls State University from which he graduated with an excellent academic record. I guess I expected more of a businessman or professional type, but why should I? Is anyone in our family normal (other than me)?

We nicknamed both Rob and Heidi "Flower," because they had such a distinctive smell. Original scent! I thought that Bumper and I were kind of back woods people living in a cabin by a lake, but compared to what was in front of me, I felt like a "social debutante!" He was extremely likable, so we thought that, except for the smell, he was OK. I figured that he would last about as long as the other guys she had brought home, but wasn't too sure this time. Most of them had tried to make a good impression on their girlfriend's parents, but not Rob, he would always be himself! Hadn't I said that about Merri? Oh well, what will be, will be! At least he was not lazy, or on drugs. We figured he was probably very nice and had been well brought up.

Life back in our cabin was difficult for me, because by now, I had gotten used to Edina, and all the city things it had to offer. I was also used to a dishwasher, laundry room in the same building, swimming pool, parks, Second Chance for Life meetings and everything I would ever need within a few blocks. I was rather homesick to get back to the cocoon.

Most people who have to leave home due to illness are elated when it is time to go back home. I felt I was not normal, because getting homesick for a place you hadn't lived in for more than a few months troubled me. Maybe it was because all I had known in our little house was sickness, and it was in Edina that I had gotten to know a healthy husband.

We made the decision to sell the house and move back to Edina. Our kids were not living in Zimmerman anymore, the Barber Shop was in a real slump and we both felt we were ready for a move.

I felt badly about telling the Jednecks that I was considering leaving, because they had let me keep all my stuff in the shop, without paying rent, during the time I was gone. They were wonderful about it, and didn't blame us for wanting to move.

I called a realtor to come look at the house. We decided that if we could sell it, we could use that money to put down on a condo in the city.

I let my sister know what our plans were, and a couple of days later, Harvey called and wanted me to send him my tax statements from the previous year. I had hardly worked that year because of Bumper's health and of moving to the cocoon. I told him I was embarrassed to send it, but if he didn't laugh, I would.

After he received my tax statements, which looked like we were in the middle of the big depression, he called and told me to go look at condos and call him when I found one. I wasn't sure why, but, we went looking and found one we liked in a short time.

Lori and Harvey flew in from Chicago to look at what we had picked out, and Harvey told the realtor that we wanted to close on it that very same day. Our realtor, and the realtor selling the condo, worked harder than they had ever worked in their lives, to do all that in one day.

By the time Lori and Harvey's plane took off for Chicago that evening, we had a new home in Edina. God had picked out my relatives!

EDINA, HERE WE COME AGAIN!

Moving this time was an exciting and fun experience. We were starting a new, healthy life in our new home, one year after Bumper's transplant operation in November of 1989.

David must have practiced, because nothing went wrong in the second move. I do have to believe that on the first move to Edina, everyone was nervous and scared, so that is probably why everything went so wrong.

Our new home was beautiful, with two sliding glass doors opening to a balcony from the large living room, dining room combination. Two bathrooms made it seem like a palace after having six of us share one bath at our old place. We now had central air, a dishwasher, a washer and dryer, everything that our cabin in the woods did not.

Like the apartment, I hadn't collected all the junk that goes with my style of every day living, so the new place was still neat and roomy.

Our condo, located almost across the street from the huge Southdale Shopping Center, was close to everything. If I ever win the lottery, get rich and full of wrinkles, a plastic surgeon has an office across the street, with the hospital next door. If I were a hiking nut, I could get everywhere without a car, but I think I prefer the wheels.

As soon as we got settled in, Lori called and wanted me to go to Palm Springs, California. She thought it would be fun for me to have a vacation, and go house hunting with her. My life was getting so exciting. Bumper was well now, so Mother-in-Law could check on him. Lori, coming from Chicago, and me from Minneapolis, were going to meet in Denver to change planes. I boarded the plane that we were both supposed to be on, but Lori wasn't there so I got on the plane, sure in the knowledge that my sister would stop it from taking off, because my sister is almost capable of moving mountains. I was stunned when the plane left without her.

Her plane was late getting in, so I was stranded in Palm Springs until the next flight came in. I called her realtor to tell him that she would be in later, and he offered me a car to use until then. I hadn't heard of anyone doing that, but I said "No thank you", because where would I go? I amused myself "people watching" until I saw her hurried little figure running toward me.

She had rooms for us at a resort, so I lived in luxury the next few days. I felt quite important looking at the most beautiful homes I had ever seen, and being with my sister. Maybe people thought I was rich enough to live in one of those beauties.

I was there when she picked out their first home in Palm Springs! Coming home to the new condo was nice, because it still was uncluttered.

Two weeks later, I got another phone call, saying we should get one of the boys, rent a truck, and come to Chicago to pick up the furniture they wouldn't be taking to Palm Springs. Furniture from their beautiful mansion…absolutely!

Whatever they didn't want, I could take, but she said that the kids and I could all pick out what we wanted. I wanted it all, but knew our condo couldn't hold it. I guess I would share a little!

Jon brought Kayla, about two years old, and the four of us left for the windy city. We brought back a big truck full of wonderful treasures that I had to share. I had by this time become stingy!

Our new living room looked even more elegant with our newly acquired antique, French Provincial, three-piece sofa that took a whole corner of the room, plus more. On the table in back of it is a beautiful, tall French lamp, with a nude statue on it. In front of the sofa is an antique, marble table. On the wall by it are beautiful antique pictures and things from the mansion wall. Also, we have huge mirrors on other walls. We looked like we belonged in Edina with our beautiful furnishings. Sometimes looks are deceiving, but what the heck, we could fool them all!

Our next surprise, a week later, was from Harvey, telling us he was giving a surprise birthday party for Lori in July, and the whole family was to come. I almost fell off our beautiful sofa when he said it would be in Jerusalem, Israel, and I should tell all of the kids, as they were invited too. This was January, so in six months, we would all be going to Israel. He also told me it was a surprise party! That news was fun to spread throughout the family! Bumper, the one that feared the dentist, and would rather have a transplant than go to the dentist, was also scared of flying. Tough! He was going to get on that plane anyway, and I let him know it!

Having the time of our lives, and being so involved with Second Chance, still didn't alter the fact that I had to find a job. A small town barber can't compete with big city ones, and if I were to work for someone else, I would have to do women's hair, which I do not do. I decided to take a job in an up-scale grocery store in Edina, on France Avenue. I would get my health insurance and paid vacations, so Byerly's grocery turned out to be the place for me. I still did barbering, but at the University Hospital, for long-term "organ waiters." In the hospital, I did cut women's hair, but that is not like doing it in a shop, working for someone else.

I was living like I was retired, except for going to work. I chose a "five in the morning" shift, so I would have all afternoon free.

Life was getting more exciting every day!

ISRAEL

Our new title was beginning to take form when Harvey took the whole family to Israel for Lori's birthday party. No one could top the title, because what was in our future was not possible on the money we had. We will always hold the title we bestowed on ourselves, which is, "THE WORLD'S POOREST JET SETTERS".

Our family, Sonja, husband Marty, Jon (Merri had to stay home due to illness), divorced Randy, and Heidi, all met us at the Minneapolis airport. Daniel, Kirsten, and Kayla being so small stayed home.

Bumper was excited to go, and being only 18 months out of heart transplant made it extra special. He had this fear of flying, so the doctors gave him Valium, but he still had qualms about setting foot on the plane. I was very annoyed and said to him "Get on the damn plane". "If God wanted you dead, He had every chance to take you, so quit your belly-aching and get on the damn plane". He did, and that, along with Valium helped his recovery from his FEAR OF FLYING!

At Kennedy Airport in New York, we met Lori and Harvey; their daughter Subie, husband Al, and kids, from St. Louis; Harvey's mother Lilian; and his brother and wife, Stanley and Maryanne, all from Florida.

Boarding the airplane in New York was a little traumatic for Bumper again, but he didn't dare act like too much of a baby with all the added people of the family. I just told him to take his Valium and shut up. It worked.

On the flight, my family all felt like we belonged to royalty, because how many people have a re-union or birthday party, with all expenses paid, to visit a foreign land and stay at a first class hotel? We felt as if we belonged to a powerful multi-millionaire family, and then started laughing, because we do!

It was impossible to keep a big trip with the whole family coming a secret forever, so Lori already knew about her surprise birthday party, but didn't know what it would be.

Landing in Israel, we were met by Lori and Harvey's other daughter Kyra, and her husband Momo, and their family, who live in Israel. Momo is a Sabra, which means a Jewish person born in Israel.

We stayed in the nicest hotel in Jerusalem, and they also had vans to take us site seeing through the whole country of Israel.

The second day we were there, we heard about the take-over of Kuwait when we were in the elevator. That was scary news for Israel. It made our trip tourist free, because most Americans left immediately. The Dome of the Rock, Calvary, Massada, and other tourist places were deserted. We saw the Western Wall, site of the six-day war, Jericho and Bethlehem. The spot where Jesus was born was empty except for us.

The birthday party was the most expensive and elegant bash we had ever been to. Lori came into the private dining room in a horse drawn carriage. She was surprised when Harvey had the carriage brought to the back door of the hotel, and they drove right through the hotel. A band played God Save the Queen or something like that as the carriage entered the room. Onlookers could see a little bit of what was going on, and they must have believed we really were the Royal Family, and by now, I was sure of it!

The cocktail hour featured a harpist playing, and was held on the hotel's roof overlooking all of Jerusalem. From there, Harvey took Lori to board the carriage, while we all went to a dining room.

Never have I seen such an assortment of food so well displayed. This party was for sure the most expensive affair I had ever been to. Never had I felt so important, or that I belonged to such a distinguished family. The party ended with movies from Lori's childhood, and dancing the Hora.

Leaving the hotel the next day, we traveled throughout the country. The Dead Sea was wonderful and fun. I tried to see if I could drown in it, but since it is impossible to submerge, it is also impossible to drown. Randy had gotten into poison ivy before the trip and had it all over his body, so was in misery. When he went into the Dead Sea, his body burned, and the poison ivy was gone. He felt relief from all his pain and itching. We spent an evening on a kibbutz where Momo's relatives lived. We headed north to a resort on the Lebanon border. I was a little scared when I looked out the window in our room, and there was Lebanon. We saw Haifa, Sea of Galilee, Tel Aviv, all of Israel. What a wonderful trip!

When it was time to end our beautiful vacation, getting out of the country was a problem, because all the flights had stopped coming in. We had to leave at different times, and the only way Harvey could get us out was to fly El Al to Frankfurt, and then back to the U.S. It was in Frankfurt I learned that El Al planes never come up to the terminals for security reasons. We were well guarded.

That was an unforgettable birthday party and re-union. I belong to a good family!

THE ARRIVAL OF ARI

The University Hospital did not accept normal, uncomplicated births, so it was normal for someone in our family to be born there.

With Sonja's rare three-chamber heart, no one with a heart identical to hers had ever given birth. Although there have been a few other women with similar conditions, they were not identical to hers. The doctors informed us that theoretically everything should work out fine. We were all terrified.

The baby wanted to make a very early appearance at 30 weeks gestation, so Sonja was put in the hospital for two weeks to forestall the delivery, while they gave her shots and medicine to make the baby's lungs develop.

The very small maternity section was located in a corner of the fifth floor of the old hospital, which was the Mayo Building. The fifth floor was where they kept the mothers and infants after birth. They put her in an attic-like area where the labor rooms were, and that is where she stayed until the birth. It was cramped and small. Usually one wouldn't stay in the labor rooms for more than a couple of days, but they wanted her near the operating room in case the baby came.

On some days, there would be policemen in front of the labor rooms, and I asked one of them why? " Many of the women that give birth here are on crack," was his answer. I said, "but why are YOU here?" "Because they may get up and walk away" he said. "In labor?" "Yes, on crack they could get up and walk out" he said.

I felt so sorry for Sonja having to stay in that tiny room. Little Ariel decided to make his appearance 8 weeks early, on November 25,1990. Randy's girl, Kirsten, was also born on November 25, four years earlier, so at least that would make it easier to remember their birthdays.

When Sonja was wheeled into the operating room, there were three medical teams waiting for her; one for her heart, one a premature birth team, and a pediatric team. Add to that nurses, anesthesiologists, and other medical personnel, and there had to be over twenty people in the room.

Even with all the help in the world available, we still worried about Sonja.

Ari made his big entrance weighing four pounds, one ounce. He spent a few weeks in neo-natal intensive care and was the best looking baby in the incubators. That was true, because not many babies were born at the hospital, and most were from drug mothers. He was the calmest of all. It was pathetic to see all those sick little babies, and again, we had to count our blessings. Sonja and Ari were given the best care anyone could have had. Ari was so tiny that I was afraid to touch him when he came home with his parents.

When Sonja decided it was time to return to work, a company that was owned by an airline employed her, which meant that her parents could fly at discounted rates.

We were already working on our title "World's Poorest Jet Setters". We would fly off someplace every time I could get days off in a row from work. For my birthday that year, we flew to Philadelphia for lunch.

Once we were going to go to Las Vegas, but the plane was full, so we jumped on a plane for San Diego, and had a marvelous couple of days. We had never had so much fun in our lives.

HEIDI AND THE HIPPIE PAD

In the spring, Heidi excitedly called and wanted us to see the place in Wisconsin that she was renting with some friends, Rob included. It was out in the middle of nowhere, which, knowing Heidi, didn't shock us.

Following the directions given us, ahead of us we saw the worst structure we had ever seen on barren, treeless land. Quietly, almost in a tone of prayer, I said to Bumper, "That couldn't be it, could it? I hope not, but I think it is". In unison we said, "OH MY GOD!" Bumper said, "Maybe we are on the wrong road, this looks like the city dump. If railroad tracks ran along side of it, the place would be perfect for a hobo convention". Driving up the long rutted road, my hopes were that it would look better close up.

Reaching the structure, we found it looked even worse up close. Being greeted by Rob's coon hounds, I was afraid to step out of the car, but Heidi said they were friendly. Coon hounds shouldn't have surprised me, because Rob was a hunter, trapper and woodsman who preferred to stay away from cities. I was hoping her infatuation with this creature of the wilderness would be a mirage, and leave with the morning fog like her other boyfriends. Even the Spanish guy with three kids didn't sound too bad at the moment.

Heidi greeted us, excited to give us a tour of her new house. I think it was a relic left over from the 1960 hippie era. The only thing missing was a purple van with yellow flowers painted on it, sitting outside the awful looking trailer house. Entering the kitchen through a door that was loose and held together by leather hinges, we met her friends. They sort of matched the house. I knew they were nice kids, so that must account for something. Leading me through the small trailer with a couple of annexes built onto it, I was afraid for her safety, because it looked like a tinderbox. Even if the fire department was next door, I didn't think they would be able to save it. I was having a silent panic attack thinking of her sleeping in a trap like that, but was as nice as I could be about warning her of the dangers.

Even living far out in the country, with no locks wasn't very smart, but I knew a burglar would have no interest in such a place. We thought of buying her a tent, because it would be safer and just as burglar proof.

If I thought the main house was bad, Bumper and I were both surprised when we discovered that the back of the trailer was dug out from a hill, and there was a big dog house under the house made especially for Rob's coon hounds.

She liked this place? I thought I had done a good job of raising kids, but now I was feeling a little inferior about the job I had done. What more can a mother do? We didn't stay too long, we just wished her happiness, and asked if maybe they could find a little safer place in which to live?

One daughter lived a nutty existence and one daughter challenged medical history. Where had I gone wrong?

If Randy could find a nice, new wife, if Merri didn't have severe diabetes, if Sonja's heart condition didn't challenge medical history and if Heidi would choose civilization, I think my life could be almost normal!

HEARST CASTLE JUNIOR

Lori and Harvey bought a second home in Palm Springs, called Hearst Castle Junior. The original owner of the house had been the late George Randolph Hearst and his wife Rosalie. Harvey and Lori bought it from a man who had painted the beautiful rooms black. After he made a mess of it, he decided to sell it, because when it went up for sale, my sister was fast on the scene.

I hadn't seen the house before she redid it, but my sister restored it to the elegance of the Hearst family era.

Mrs. Hearst wanted to see what her home looked like after the new owners had restored it, so she called Lori from her home she had built just down the mountain from her previous home.

I couldn't believe that my sister was nervous about meeting anyone, but Harvey said she was scared and excited when Mrs. Hearst was on the way over.

When she looked at the beautiful mansion and saw that my sister had restored it in the very same colors that had been in the house before, and saw that it looked as elegant as it had when she lived in it, they became the closest of friends. In fact, friends for life!

I didn't know much about the home until Lori sent me a video of the estate. Bumper and I sat and watched what was to be the beginning of our exciting life to come.

As I looked at the spacious, elegant rooms, I couldn't believe I knew anyone that lived in such splendor. One side of the house had windows overlooking the Coachella Valley; the large swimming pool was similar to the one at San Simeon, the Hearst Castle between L.A. and San Francisco. Bumper and I were in a state of shock looking at pictures of the estate that had been home to stars, royalty, the Hearst family, and my sister! I knew Harvey was well to do, but this was far beyond my imagination.

I knew that I would someday see the house, even sleep in the house, but I didn't know it would help to mold the way our lives were changing, and to what degree.

Being rather a country hick, I also had fears about whether my sister would invite me. She had been grooming me for many years to be proper and charming, but so far, I had flunked the courses. I knew I had to get serious, remember all the proper English and Finishing School tactics she had tried to teach me. Maybe I was beginning to figure out why she had been grooming me all my life. I could not go to Palm Springs if I would be an embarrassment to them. Oh Lord! And then we have Bumper, who can very easily resemble a bull in a china shop. The more I thought, the more worried I became. Would I ever meet Mrs. Hearst? I didn't think so. I thought maybe my sister would hide me in the closet if Mrs. Hearst were to come to the door. My mind was in a dangerous mood, running into places it shouldn't be. I couldn't be as insecure and backwoods as I was making myself to be, could I?

THANKSGIVING IN PALM SPRINGS

With Sonja having a job with the airline, it was possible for us to fly in and out of Palm Springs, or the surrounding cities, whenever the desire hit us.

When we were invited for the first time to Hearst Castle Junior, it was for Thanksgiving weekend, and we were excited! Harvey's mother Lillian, brother Stanley and his wife Maryann, would also be coming, but we didn't know who the rest of the guests would be, which was a good thing. We were invited to a formal Ball the Sunday night after Thanksgiving. Finding proper apparel to wear was a challenge for us. We were busy trying to make ourselves look like we belonged there.

Juggling a work schedule in a grocery store deli, and flying off to live with the rich and famous was not easy, but I became good at my own motto, "I led two lives".

Getting to the Palm Springs home, Bumper and I wandered around in complete awe for what must have been an hour. The first thing we saw when we went through the front door was a large fishpond, which in my state of mind, I almost fell in to. From there, both large living rooms are all windows and mirrors. The dining room was also windows and mirrors and all of the rooms overlook the valley, mountains and pool. I could barely sleep that night due to the excitement of sleeping in such splendor.

In our bedroom, I found some pretty clothes hanging on hangers near the closet, my size. I knew that the clothes didn't fit my sister, and that she had bought them for me. She always did worry about what my wardrobe would be, so she wanted me to look good enough to at least get to a store if I brought some of my outlandish things. One thing she absolutely hates are my gopher feet earrings, which happen to be my favorite. I sent the same earrings to her daughter Subie, because we have the same taste, and that worries my poor sister.

The clothing also came in handy, because coming the night before Thanksgiving, we couldn't have gone to a store, so I had to look good for the guests. Who were the guests? Mrs. Hearst! Panic was setting in and Lori hadn't told me I would have to eat in the closet! I could eat at the table with everyone else. Bumper wasn't scared, because he just doesn't worry about huge things like that. He wouldn't care who was coming for dinner, as long as there is enough food. I was worrying all by myself.

Lori told me to just be myself, but to be kind of quiet. How can I be myself and be quiet? I am a loudmouth! As scared as I was, maybe being quiet would be easy for once.

William, the Estate Manager, is also the Cook, Chauffeur, and keeps the house running. He was wonderful and told me not to worry. I was just calming down a bit when he broke the news that one of the other guests would be W.P. Kinsella, who was the author of SHOELESS JOE, which became the movie FIELD OF DREAMS, which I had just seen. Oh my God!

I didn't have time to worry about whether or not our grown kids at home were eating a decent meal. They were all together except Heidi, who was now living in the Teton Mountains of Wyoming with Rob. They would probably be eating moose or something, since they are both hunters. They would all have to fend for themselves without mother. I had enough problems of my own just getting through Thanksgiving. How could I act like myself? Maybe Lori wanted me to act like someone else! I thought that if she wanted me to be quiet, I would try to do that. I would talk only when I was asked something. I hoped they wouldn't ask me where I worked. I was a barber, and I do cut hair at the hospital. I could tell them that. I do live in Edina, and maybe they would know that it is an exclusive suburb. They wouldn't know that! Bumper having had a heart transplant, that is what we could talk about! After talking to myself for at least half an hour, I was getting stressed out and talked out, so maybe I could shut up!

Guests started arriving. I was calm and collected. They were all very rich and very nice. William answered the door and in camc W.P.Kinsella, who put me at ease right away. He was very casual, wearing jeans and long unkempt hair, but I couldn't help but like him right off the bat. His girlfriend was with him, and she was very much like him. Lovable and laughable, that was Bill Kinsella.

When I was starting to relax, who came next? Mrs. Hearst, with Tom O'Sullivan, her lifelong friend and escort. I was in complete awe of her. She was beautiful, walking proud, and put you immediately at ease by her kind ways. It took me only a few minutes to realize this was a very nice lady, and that I was no longer afraid of her.

The help served the good dinner, and Bill Kinsella kept us laughing through out the meal.

By the end of the day, I had acquired a wonderful new friend by the name of Rosalie Hearst, and knew W.P. Kinsella as Bill.

I hadn't heard any bad news, so the kids must have survived Thanksgiving without me!

OUR FIRST CHARITY BALL

We were nervous about the Charity Ball held two days after Thanksgiving. It was something new to us, and we knew celebrities and rich and important people would be there. We normally hang out more with the popcorn and hot dog kind of people.

I had found a beautiful dress at the fat lady's store, where I am a petite size, and Bumper had bought a tuxedo. Our clothes would look all right; we just had to watch how we acted.

As we were dressing, Bumper could not find his bow tie. After looking through everything, he knew he must have left it at home, but was surprised because he knew he had packed all of it together. He borrowed one from Harvey, and off we went to the Ball.

Entering the elegant room, we were glad to know we would sit at a table of ten with Stanley and Maryanne (Harvey's brother and sister-in-law), and a group of fun people. Lori and Harvey and Rosalie Hearst sat at a different table with very close friends. As soon as Bumper sat down, he knew where his bow tie was- in the crotch of his pants! He mentioned where it was and the gay beautician next to him offered to get it out, but Bumper said he could manage. That cracked up the entire table.

Eddie, the gay beautician was an escort, so he bitched all night because he had to wear a Tux, when he wanted to dress in drag. When a beautiful gown would go by, Eddie would exclaim, "That would look much better on me." He had a fetish for feet and was jealous of all the glittery shoes. I knew he would probably look great as a girl. He sure seemed like one. He had to go to the bathroom so he said to Bumper, "I have to go to the little room, and

I'll be back unless I fall in love." He kept the whole table in stitches.

I couldn't believe I was quiet, but I was too busy "people watching" to see if anyone looked familiar.

One man looked exactly like Paul Newman, and it was his brother. George Montgomery (from a few years back) was there, along with other older stars, which made me feel like I was at a Hollywood bash.

I was wishing all my friends could see me now! I was in no hurry to get back to work at the grocery store, but I was excited to relate all the exciting events, knowing nobody in their right mind would believe me anyway.

When the magical night was almost over, I was trying to locate my new sparkle shoes that I had carefully slipped off during dinner. I presumed they would stay near my feet, but for some strange reason, they had moved. Did Bumper accidentally or on purpose kick them? Did the good fairy at this magical affair take them? What would I do to find them? What else COULD I do but go under the table and find them! I crawled on all fours under the table, peeked out and saw William, who was also at our table, laughing at me. Of course, he told all the others, so I was quite the Belle of the Ball peering out from under the tablecloth on all fours. I had two choices, should I be embarrassed and cry? Or should I just say "The hell with it" and laugh? I chose the latter and soon, it didn't seem so embarrassing!

That was the end of our Thanksgiving weekend at Hearst Castle Junior. I knew when I got back to work, I would be unhappy, and crash dive off my pedestal. I knew I would fall on my head and ass, and it would take days to get over my fall from Glory.

That was the start of "I Lead Two Lives."

THE COWBOY WEDDING

About a year before the wedding in 1994, Heidi and Rob decided they wanted to live in the mountains, so Rob went off to Wyoming to find a job and a place to live. Soon Heidi followed and the lifestyle they chose began. Rob and Heidi set the date for their wedding and of course, planned a unique one! When the time arrived, Bumper and I flew to Wyoming for the big occasion.

We arrived a day early and were told to go up to Bonderant, a small town up in the mountains from Jackson Hole. They were living in a very tiny cabin, but if they were not home when we got there, we should go to the bar and ask for Sam, the Cowboy who was in charge of the Chuck Wagon dinner for the reception.

Knowing they were caretakers for an old lodge with a few dilapidated cabins that had served as a whorehouse years ago, I was sure I spotted the cabin right next to the lodge.

I was a little apprehensive opening the door, but as soon as I saw my old Norwegian coffee pot on the stove, I knew we had the right place. It was a lot better than the old trailer house they had once lived in, as this was the size of a double outhouse. Why didn't that surprise me?

Since they weren't home, we decided to go on up to the bar and find Sam! That was easy because only one customer was in the bar, and by his clothes and handlebar mustache, we knew it had to be Sam.

We had heard about Sam, so, before we left home, Bumper decided to see whether or not Sam had a sense of humor. Walking up to the man at the bar, Bumper said "You Sam?" "Yeah." "I'm here to pay you for the pig roast tomorrow." "Yeah, she said you were coming sometime." "Do you care if I pay you in two dollar bills?" Without changing expression or a look of surprise, Sam said "Pay me any way you want, or you can even pay me later." "No, I'll pay you now." Then Bumper hauled out a BIG roll of two-dollar bills and counted out all the money for the pig. I was hidden, laughing, and trying to hold my camera straight. Sam sat with no expression on his face, just looked at the money that was counted out, picked it up, rolled it all in his top pocket, and said "Thank you." Knowing he was not the most talkative soul in the world, we felt we knew him well by now!

The groom's dinner was held at an appropriate place called Horse Creek Inn. It was there that I met a new life friend, Heidi's new mother-in-law, Ellie.

We stayed at a hotel in Jackson Hole, but most of the guests, their college friends and the younger crowd, either camped by the lodge or rented cabins near-by.

The dawn of a perfect day for a wedding started out with the under blouse to go under my western top not fitting. The tag had said the right size, so I had bought it. Wonderful, what to do? I just cut the back and pinned it. Now, that was over so nothing else could go wrong.

The minister had to come from 200 miles away to marry them, because the tiny church in the mountains had no minister. We didn't know it was his first wedding. The church was packed, so half of the friends had to stand outside, along with the Harley bikes of some of the cowboys. Sitting in the tiny church, my fear left me, because this wedding would go off just fine.

Heidi wanted Bumper and her dad, (my ex), to walk her down the aisle. Thank God it was a short walk, because the tiny church had a narrow aisle, and Bumper was large, my ex was getting drunk, and poor Heidi was squashed in the middle. The minister started to marry them, but we all noticed that something was missing, the groom. The young minister had put him in a back room. The door of the room had locked, and he forgot to go and get him.

When the wedding started and the minister started to marry my daughter with the groom's brother, the stand-in groom ran out, and got Rob out of his cell. Everyone clapped. Nothing else could go wrong now! Just after the minister said, "A man shall leave his wife, to take a wife", Daniel, our grandson, now ten, had to throw up, so he went running out the door. The ceremony continued, and the minister blessed the beer top rings, that some friend had snuck in, instead of the real rings. A woman was supposed to sing, but the tape broke, so there was no music.

Bumper and my ex were supposed to be seated after the ceremony started, but the minister forgot to tell them to sit down, so they stood up at the tiny altar throughout the wedding. I was hoping both of them would remain standing upright, because Bumper was getting a little tired, and ex was drunk. There was no seating left for them anyway. The minister asked Sonja to give communion and she just stood and stared for a few minutes. She had no idea what to do. He quickly told her how to do the job, and she did it, but not without a few laughs from the crowd. At the end of the ceremony, the adorable minister screwed up the words to the Lord's Prayer. A very fitting end for a very different wedding!

I couldn't believe that Bumper had changed into his shorts and tee shirt right in the church hall after the ceremony, but since most of the guests wore western clothes and jeans, I just shrugged and gave in.

Two modern things at the wedding were the Limo and the Harley Bikes. The bridal party went down to Jackson in the Limo to hit a bar or two, so everyone else went to get acquainted in the Lodge next to the cabin. Heidi and Rob had gotten permission to use the Lodge, free of charge, but they had to clean it up. The bullet holes in the wall of the bar were noticeable. I guess six people had been shot there, so it had been closed years before. It was rustic and quite a good spot. Sonja had gotten married the first time in the Zoo, so for Heidi to get married in an old whorehouse made perfect sense to me.

The wedding party hadn't yet arrived when the chuck wagon food was ready, so I told the crowd, "Let's eat, we don't need them!" While we were eating, the wedding party returned. I was surprised when I saw how many people were crammed into the limo. Ex husband was the first one to tumble out, with poor Maryanne, wife # 3 holding him up. I guess he had been the bartender, testing everyone's drink to make sure they wouldn't get sick. He always was KIND that way.

The locals of the small mountain town had come with their dogs and kids, and I almost fell over a large dog lying placidly amid the crowd. After catching my fall, I found out the fat man in bib overalls was the owner of the big dog. I found out the man's name was Psycho and the dog's name was DOG. That was the end of our intelligent conversation. The western band was good and everyone danced the night away.

In the morning, we came back to the lodge for the gift opening. We were a little early, and people were still sleeping all over the ground, some in tents, some not. Cowboy Jack was sleeping in the back end of a pickup, big Earl was sleeping on the ground, with his head on a saddle, and little Earl was under the truck on the bare ground sound asleep. When we entered the bar/lodge, what a sight we saw! A Harley had been set on the bar by a bunch of cowboys. The place was a disaster! It looked like what the Little Big Horn must have looked like after Custer's last Stand! The wedding cake had been covered to finish eating at the gift opening, but mice were happily scampering in and out of it. One of the guests was standing and eating some cake anyway. I was wondering if his bloodshot eyes could see the little critters, of if he had seen pink elephants before, so a few mice didn't scare him?

Heidi and Rob had spent the night in someone's motor home, and they made their appearance as we were all trying to clean up the mess. It took a lot of hung over guys to get the Harley off the bar, but maybe not so many drunks to put it up there!

After lunch, and the gift opening, the less intelligent guests went on a trail ride up the steep cliffs of the mountain. I had heard about how scary the ride was, so we wouldn't have gone on the Poker Ride anyway. It was called that because they played poker or something at some of the stops along the way. Probably instead of strip poker, it was, "Who Will Survive the Ride Poker".

We went with our niece Subie and her kids, Jon and most of our grand kids, up the mountain in a covered wagon, to a cowboy picnic.

Everyone left for home on the 4th of July. As we were leaving, we all shook our heads and agreed this was the end of a wonderful wedding. 'Everything that could go wrong did'. A wedding can't get much better than that!

LIFESTYLES OF THE RICH AND FAMOUS

Working in an upscale Deli wasn't the most fun job in the world, but when I juggled my crazy life with it, I was able to make it fun.

By this time, we were going to fancy Balls every year in Palm Springs, and I was getting to know a lot of celebrities. Bumper and I were having so much fun!

Not only were we meeting people that under normal circumstances we would never see, Harvey was sending us on trips throughout the world.

On my first big cruise, I went as a companion to Lillian, Harvey's mother, to Athens, the Greek Isles, Turkey, and across the Black Sea to Russia.

Being my first big cruise, I stood craning my neck looking at the biggest ship I had ever seen. I loved everything about the cruise except losing Lillian in Turkey. I was supposed to take care of her, and I was, until she went almost running down a street in Istanbul, when she saw a sign for a leather shop. I was looking away, and then I noticed her entering a store a little ways ahead of me.

Running into the doorway, there was no store, just two Turkish men in Fezzes standing by an elevator inside the empty room. My heart was racing. I was scared. Where could Lillian have gone? Not thinking they could even understand me, I was frantically trying to get the words to come out of my mouth, "Where's the woman that just came in here?"

One of the men said "Come with me." What? Did he expect me to get into an elevator leading who knows where, with two strange men? I was terrified, but what other choice did I have? Had Lillian been crazy enough to get into the elevator and go with them? She had to have gone, because she wasn't in this big empty room. My job was to watch Lillian, so even if the men would kill me, I would have to go, because if I didn't, I would get killed for not getting her. Which death did I prefer?

Again the man said "Come, I will take you to her." In silence I got in, and was thinking that maybe she was already dead, or we would die together. The elevator opened into a large, empty warehouse, and seeing that, I was close to wetting my pants. The man said, "Come." At that moment, I thought I knew what men on death row feel like when they take the final walk. He opened a large door, and there was a department store, and there was Lillian looking at leather skirts right next to the door. I didn't know if I should laugh or cry, but before I did anything, I would have to find a bathroom. To this day, I cannot understand how Lillian would dare to go up the elevator with those men.

After that, Harvey started sending both Bumper and me on cruises and land trips.

On every vacation from the store, I would travel off to some exotic place on earth, and by then, the friends close to me knew I was telling the truth. Some, at first, just thought I was going to a mental hospital, but then I hadn't improved much when I returned. That was half the fun, keeping them guessing.

Harvey bought Lori a Bentley, so when we arrived in Palm Springs, we would now be picked up in style! Most of the time we would fly into Ontario, California on our cheap tickets, and William would come and pick us up in the Bentley. My head was getting even bigger now! I would tell the girls at work, "I'm going to Hearst Castle Junior to mingle with the rich and famous, and William will pick me up in the Bentley." "Sure you are." They had a little trouble swallowing that one, until I took a picture of William and me in the Bentley and hung it in the employee room, and gave one to the store manager. At least they could think about it now!

SAN SIMEON

On a Thursday afternoon in the middle of October 1994, I answered the phone to the sweetest call I have ever received. "Would I like to spend a week at the working ranch of the Hearst Family below San Simeon?" Harvey was the caller, and he couldn't go, so I could share a room with my sister, and Rosalie would like me to come.

"Of course I would love to go! Who wouldn't?" "You will have to fly out to Ontario in the morning, and William will pick you up at the airport. Think you can get on the plane?" "I'll be there, and if the flight is full, I'll call you right away and get on the next one".

Thursday was my day off, and I was to start my vacation on Saturday, so all I had to worry about was Friday. I decided that I would call in and tell them I could not be in to work the next day. The boss wasn't there, so I left a message that I wouldn't be there. I didn't tell them the reason, because I knew they would not believe me anyway, and no one from around here had heard of the working Ranch below the Castle, where the Hearst family goes for a vacation. The Castle was given to the State, but the family still owned the Ranch. I would tell my boss why I couldn't make it when I got home.

What was I going to do and say at the Ranch? What was I going to wear? I had to get to the beauty shop if I was to leave the next day. I also had to get to the fat lady's store to get something that I would look slim and wonderful in, maybe even a couple of things. Those things kept me busy the rest of the day so I wouldn't worry so much. I wished I had known about the trip earlier, but then, I was glad I hadn't, because that would have been more stress than I wanted to handle. Was all the stress of being on the Hearst Ranch for a week worth it? HELL, YES! I would have to keep my mouth shut for the rest of the day, because no one except Bumper would know I was not insane, thinking I was going to a real Castle, with someone from the real Hearst Family. Bumper told the kids and Mother-in-Law, because they knew it was true.

Because of Sonja's good job, we ran out to her office and got tickets to California and back. The flight looked good for the next morning, so I was ready to go, except for the fact that I didn't look good in anything, even the new outfit I had just bought. A slim person could get something out of a trash bin and look good, but heavier ones, like me can look bad in a designer outfit. I was ready, except for the fact that I was scared out of my wits, and at the same time I was excited to go.

Sleep never did come to me because of the excitement and fear of making a fool of myself. I didn't need the alarm, because I was still tossing and turning and worrying when it went off early that morning. My boss had tried to call me the night before, but I didn't pick up the answering machine, because I knew she would probably tell me I couldn't go, since my vacation started on Saturday. If I didn't pick it up, I wouldn't have to deal with it, because nothing was going to stop me from going on this trip. Grocery store jobs are a dime a dozen, but going to San Simeon is not an everyday occurrence for anyone, especially me. If I had told the boss, they would maybe let me out on a mental leave, which would be O.K. too.

Bumper knew how scared I was when I was quiet in the car going to the airport. He kept trying to assure me that I had all the grace and charm that was needed, and Rosalie would love me for myself. I knew Rosalie liked me, but she hadn't spent a whole week with me. I was bound to screw up and embarrass my sister somewhere along the way. Bumper's words did not console me much. I knew I was the luckiest person in the world to get this great chance, but fear and wonderful chances often go together.

On the airplane, I put on my fake nails, which was the one thing I didn't have time to do in the excitement and flurry of getting ready. Things were going quite well, until the glue slipped, and my finger was stuck very, very hard to the little eating table connected to the seat. The man next to me had a big grin on his face, but I didn't think it was funny. After a long and painful time, I got my finger free. Then I had to polish them. The man next to me took it all in stride, and said that he liked the smell of polish. "It reminds me of my wife." He said. Was his wife dead or something? Maybe that was why he liked it? I was picked up by William in the Bentley and headed for Palm Springs. The next day we would drive up to San Simeon, which is way north of L.A.

As soon as I saw Lori, she said, "Let's go shopping." Wonderful words! Maybe she could find something that made me look like I weighed 100 pounds. Maybe she could figure out some way to make me look like the beauty queen I so desired to be. My sister could do most anything, but even in the magical world I lived in, I didn't think she could accomplish that. Oh well, at least she could improve me.

Another night of fitful sleep waiting to go to San Simeon. I felt like I had to be a good actress to pull off all this mingling with the rich and famous.

THE ROAD TO SAN SIMEON

Rosalie and Gladys, her secretary, went together in one car; Gladys drove Rosalie's Cadillac and Lori and I went in the Bentley. We left Palm Springs early in the morning, because it's a long trip to San Simeon. The Castle is between Los Angeles and San Francisco.

We brought bag lunches with us, and through the car phones, someone suggested we stop and eat our lunch at a truck stop just north of L.A. That sounded good to all of us, so we pulled the two nice cars into the rest area. The rest stop was full of people picnicking and sitting around. It looked like the melting pot of all nations.

I knew Bentleys were classy, but when I opened the trunk, I found out that this one had a place for a tablecloth and picnic supplies. Built in!

The four of us looked wealthy, not only because the cars, but because of all the jewelry we were wearing. I had borrowed some of my sister's, so that I could pass for rich and famous, too.

One of us should have had second thoughts when the League of Nations began circling the cars, admiring them.

We found a table and sat with our lunches. I soon began thinking this was a pretty stupid place to be sitting with Rosalie Hearst! It would have been a good place for a kidnapping. With the jewelry alone, any one of the admirers could have lived easily for the rest of his life, even if he were young.

As thoughts of how stupid we were ran through my head, the others must have been getting the same pictures too, because we decided to hurry and finish our food. Gladys was allergic to bees, and they were also joining the League of Nations around us. We very quickly packed up and left. I think that was a good idea. People were watching us leave. That was the only time I have had a picnic at an L.A. rest area, and I also think it will be my last.

Heading north along the coast was a beautiful trip, made even better by riding in a Bentley. It is also fun to have people look at you and think you are rich and famous, when the opposite is true.

Highway #1 took us through beautiful little towns such as San Luis Obispo and Cambria.

Soon, La Cuesta Encantada or "The Enchanted Hill" appeared, and the beauty of the castle could be seen for miles around. Lori must have noticed that I was silent, as we drove close and passed by the Castle.

Just beyond the Castle, we turned on a private road to the right, and drove through a gate saying, Rancho Piedra Blanca, which was the name given to the Ranch that had been owned by William Randolph Hearst's parents, George and Phoebe Hearst.

At the end of the driveway was a beautiful old farm mansion, built in the 1870's. Surrounding the home was a white picket fence. There was also a huge guesthouse, a barn, and an airport. I felt very special and important, because everyone in our party was staying in the main house with Rosalie.

Going through every room in that beautiful home, made me think of the home in 'Gone with the Wind.'

Climbing the long front staircase to go to bed that night, I knew I WAS someone special, because I had been so blessed! I knew God loved me, and my sister loved me!

THE GLORY DAYS

Poor Bumper couldn't share one of the greatest memories of all time, San Simeon and the ranch. Meals at the ranch were always buffet style, with a very much down home atmosphere. I felt like I was on another planet, just looking in at the scene around me. Rosalie's best friends were there. How did I end up with all these distinguished people? I knew I didn't belong in this crowd of people, but my acting skills were getting good, so I was getting by.

Rosalie said to us, " breakfast or brunch is at 11:00. Dinner is at 7:00. You may eat any other time you would like, but you must help yourself. Feel free to use the kitchen."

We would go up to the castle in the Bentley each day, and see a different section of it than we had the previous day. We got to use the private elevators of William Randolph Hearst, which tourists never even see.

It was a step back into time to be in the rooms where Douglas Fairbanks, Rudolph Valentino, Greta Garbo, Louis Mayer of Metro-Goldwyn- Mayer, Clark Cable, and many, many more from that wonderful era of movies, spent time and partied. I felt important, rich and famous. I would stay that way until I returned home and went back to work. Then, the fall from my pedestal would again injure my ruptured and inflated ego.

There was the town of San Simeon on the map, but there was also a tiny San Simeon across from the castle, by the ocean. The post office and general store are old and unique, probably used by the castle employees and the Hearst family.-

One day, one of the women guests wanted to see how fast a Bentley could go, and the perfect place to find out would be the runway of the airport at the ranch. I thought it might be fun to go along, until I found out she wanted to go down the runway that ended at a steep cliff. I didn't think that sounded like a good idea, so I decided to sit it out. Bumper needed me for survival, since we were not wealthy, so going over a cliff would not be in his best interest. I wasn't sure Lori knew about that little venture, but what the heck? I wasn't going to say anything!

In the evening, we would sit around the fire in the antique living room and play games and put puzzles together. I stayed on my silver lined cloud all week.

Every room had a fireplace, and every guest was a Californian who thought October was a cold month. The fireplaces were on in every bedroom. Lori would turn it on, and as soon as I thought she was asleep, I would get up and turn it off. When she thought I was asleep, she would get up and turn it on, and that went on most of the nights. Being from Minnesota, I was sweating to death. No one won, no one lost, and we just kept getting up and down.

I flew out of San Luis Obispo to L.A. at the end of my wonderful stay. Lori stayed on, and the rest of them went up to another Hearst resort spot near the Oregon border, but I couldn't be gone from my home and job any longer.

I love flying, but that little long round tin can, with one seat on each side was more than I bargained for. When the pilot got on board, he had to crouch down to tell us it would be a nice flight. There was no flight attendant, and I felt like I was sealed into this thing for the rest of eternity, which means I was scared as HELL! If Bumper had been with me, he would have refused to get on. I don't think he would have fit through the door, say nothing about the seat.

Over the crying and throwing up of the baby on its mother's lap in the seat across the aisle, I kept busy by saying prayers. Not the rosary or anything, just prayers that would be universal, as I was trying to help everyone on the plane, because our fate would be the same.

Landing in L.A. was wonderful because I was still in this world. Now, a big bird would take me to Minneapolis, and back to the sccond part of my 'I Lead Two Lives' life.

Bumper was glad to see me, but the tough fall off the stool of glory was again injuring me. I wanted to stay in my other life, not go back to the deli!

When I returned to work, I was called upstairs because of the day I called to say I wouldn't be in the next day. The manager said, "Did you say you would be sick the next day?" I told him, "I would be damn sick if I didn't go." He had no idea where I had been, so I related my week to him as he sat and stared at me. Was he thinking I was nuts? Did he think I was hallucinating? I didn't care much what he thought, but then, he smiled and said, "Next time take me with you." I guess he knew I was telling the truth!

I have had many "once in a lifetime" wonderful experiences and memories, but my trip to the Glory Land of the Hearst Castle will always be one of my fondest memories. I shall never go back to the castle, because being there the way I was, with who I was, could never be replaced or repeated. It will remain in a special place in my memory for the rest of my life.

THE MOUNTAIN FAMILY

When the kids were growing up, we lived in a tiny house with no luxuries such as dishwasher, laundry and two bathrooms. I didn't like it, but I didn't know anything different. Heidi, on the other hand, has lived in places off and on since high school with the necessities such as comfort and ease. You would think she would choose to live a life with these comforts, but instead, she chose the tough life of living in the mountains, just as they did in the days of the T.V. Walton's. Most people envy them, because they live where they want to, in a style they have chosen. They could both have better jobs in any big city, but they choose not to leave the Tetons. Rob was offered a good job in Minneapolis, but since there are few coyotes, bear, moose or buffalo, they both stuck their noses up at those offers. They buy no meat, but fish and hunt for their food. I prefer buying mine at the grocery store. I respect the way they want to live, but I do not envy them.

Sage, their first daughter, was born in 1996 and Kylie Rose arrived in 1998. It was a big surprise when, a month after Sage was born, after talking on the phone to Heidi, I opened the door of our condo, and found a baby lying in a basket in the hallway. I knew Heidi was in Wyoming, so I stared at the beautiful bundle and wondered if we were living on the wrong side of Edina or something. I calmly yelled, "Bumper, someone at the door for you." He came to the door, and we were both staring, wondering if we should let the authorities know that someone had dropped a baby off at our front door. Then, we heard giggling, and there was Heidi, with her brothers and sisters hiding around the corner "I just talked to you from your home." I said. "No, I was at the airport making sure you were home," was her reply. What a surprise and wonderful weekend that was. Bumper loved having her home too, as long as he didn't have to baby sit or change a diaper.

When they came back a year later, I gave Sage a bath, and put my big rubber rat and her babies in the tub with Sage. Heidi came in and said, "Ellie (her mother-in-law) has the same rats and gives her a bath with them too." I was appalled! Heck no! I was downright mad! There couldn't be any child in the world with two grandmas that are like me! I was so mad, I told Heidi I wanted to get to know her better, so she took me over to her mother in law's house. She did not have the array of misfit wonderful things that I do, but protruding from her ceiling were several wooden ducks, just the bottom half, looking like they were swimming in water. I cracked up laughing, and that was the beginning of our life long friendship. I didn't think it was possible to meet someone so much like me, except for my niece, but she is family. Those lucky children of our children!

Ellie's second husband, Dick, had been sick for many years. When he passed away, Rob came back for his stepfather's funeral, but Heidi had to stay in the mountains. Since Dick had been so very sick, it was a relief to them when he died, so the funeral was not as sad as one would expect. I walked up to the casket, and Rob said to me, " Reach in my inside suit pocket. I have something for you." I had asked him to get me a good luck charm to carry in my purse, since he hunts anything and everything, but I knew he wouldn't bring it to the funeral. What did he have for me? I put my hand inside his coat and found that he had brought what I wanted. Here? Knowing Rob, it shouldn't have surprised me, but it did. I was trying not to laugh out loud, but wondered how I was going to get the huge gift into my purse with no one seeing it. I grabbed it out just as fast as I could and threw it into my purse, but not without a lot of stares from the people behind me. Rob hunts wild turkeys in South Dakota, and he had brought me the turkey leg and foot I had asked him for. Not only did he bring it, he put the middle finger or toe, whichever it is, pointing straight up, so the foot is giving the bird to anyone that sees it. It was beautiful! People in the funeral line wondered about both of us, but that wasn't the first time. If things weren't bad enough, Ellie was standing at the head of the casket, and as I passed, she said to me, "His dog is in there with him." I said, " What do you mean his dog? The huge dog was running around your house just two days ago. What do you mean, your dog?" " No, not Ganon", she said. "Dick had a small dog for many years that died, and we kept his ashes on the mantle. The ashes are in the casket with Dick", she said. I still looked at her like she was cracked, but at least that made sense. Later she told me that the reason they kept the ashes was so that the dog would someday be buried with him, but she had hoped it wouldn't be for a long, long time.

My turkey foot is very important to me, and what is the difference if a person carries a rabbit foot or a turkey foot? NONE. Many people carry different good luck charms, so that doesn't necessarily make me weird. My friends have been jealous, and many have asked me to have Rob get them one, but I won't.

My mountain family is never going to reform to living in, or spending much time in a big city, so I accept that. However, I do not plan on moving in with them when I am old.

TUGGERS

December 1, 1993 our fifth grandchild was born to Jon and Merri. The mother, being a severe diabetic, was the reason for Tugger, born Taylor Jon, to be the only nine-pound preemie in an incubator. His lungs collapsed because he was four and a half weeks early. He looked like Atlas tucked in among the other tiny tots.

Most of the babies in the Children's Hospital ICU were four pounds or less, so he really stood out among the preemies.

I knew our huge little guy would be fine, because in this family, we don't get anything minor, like simple colds. He fit right into our world of medical misfits.

I took one look at the little love and knew his name had to be Tugger. Bumper and I are the only ones to call him that, so he is proud that he has a "special" name, from us.

WEDDING BELLS

Randy needed a wife, and without even realizing how desperately he needed one, he met Jeanne. A single life with two kids going between him and his ex was not a good life for him. Nothing made the entire family happier than his marriage to Jeanne.

A big beautiful perfect wedding took place. No mice, no Harley's, No novice preacher. A perfect wedding!

I was told that it would be hors d'oeuvres for the reception. Hors d'oeuvres are to me, finger food. They are something you don't fill up on. You just eat them, and act dainty and delicate. My look-a-like and act-a-like niece Subie, with husband Al, and their four kids were there, along with Kyra, MoMo and their four kids from Israel. Lori, of course, was with us, and we decided to eat something more than finger food, so we all went to McDonalds.

When we got to the reception, the table was spread with turkey, ham, beef, hot dishes, salads, desserts, and of course, the cake! Jeanne is from South Dakota, and if that spread is South Dakota hors d'oeuvres, they do it up right! There was more food than I had seen on a table for a long time. Lori, being thin and beautiful, couldn't possibly eat any more, but the rest of us did go through the line, making it seem like we were just having seconds from our first meal at McD's.

A band played, and the children were the hit of the evening with their dancing. Being a Grandma, I, of course, began to panic when Tuggers couldn't be found. No one else was worried, but I hadn't worried much all night, so instinct took over. I told the cop on duty at the door, and Tuggers was soon found, sitting under a long table, watching the celebration.

Subie flew in with a present for me, that I received in the parking lot just after the wedding. We think alike, to the point that it is eerie. She had brought, on the plane with her, a suit of armor for me. I stood there looking at the beautiful guy, wondering how to tell her that I really loved it, and that it would go so well standing next to the one I already had. She didn't think I had one, and she knew that I would love having one. I knew that I would really love having two suits of armor in my small condo!

THE WEDDING THAT WASN'T

When Sonja's marriage made in heaven came tumbling down to earth as so many marriages do, she lived the life of a very beautiful blond single, and began dating men. That lifestyle appealed to her, but one day I said, "I know you are enjoying life, but I would hate to see you live alone when you get older, so if you find a good one, don't throw him away too soon, think about it." I knew I was a success when my daughter listened to that advice. She started to talk about a 'JIM', whom I had yet to meet. I wasn't too excited, because I pictured him as being someone that wouldn't be my preference for my daughter's husband.

When I finally got the chance to meet the best of her boyfriends, he was not at all what I expected. He was someone I would never have guessed she would get serious about, but after five minutes, I knew he would someday be her husband. Although he wasn't what I expected, he had some magic quality that caught hold, and I knew he was right. First time I met him, I invited him for Christmas, which was two weeks away. Sonja was a little mad at me, because she thought it was too soon for that and he would think her pushy. How could he think <u>she</u> was pushy when I was the pushy one? I told her, "This is going to be your husband, so it is not too soon." She thought as usual, that I was nuts, but that was fine with me. She couldn't let this one slip through my fingers, I thought.

On the date of their sixth month anniversary, she said they were going out to dinner. " He is going to ask you to marry him," I said. Sonja just laughed and said, "Sure, mom."

They stopped by the next day, and without having talked to her, I said, "Let me see your hand." Jim couldn't believe that I knew he had proposed, so it was then he found out that I was a genius mom with ESP. I hope he always thinks that!

They planned a beautiful wedding for November 28, 1998, the Saturday after Thanksgiving. Although it was a second marriage, they were going to have a big wedding, with all the relatives and friends present.

As usual, we went to Palm Springs for Thanksgiving, but were not staying for the annual Wonderland Ball on the Sunday night after Thanksgiving. We would be coming home for the wedding.

Two days before Thanksgiving, Heidi, who had come back from Wyoming for the wedding, called us in Palm Springs to say that Sonja was in the hospital with a blood clot in her heart. Her rare heart is something to worry about, much more so with a clot the size of a walnut in it. The clot was caused by heart failure and atrial fibrillation (an irregular heartbeat). Having only three chambers complicated this very critical situation. My sister's daughter and family from St. Louis were already in Minnesota spending Thanksgiving with all the kids at Randy and Jeanne's. Kyra and family from Israel were in Palm Springs, with plans and tickets to come to Minnesota in time for the wedding.

We immediately hopped on a plane for home, and Kyra and family came two days later. Even if the wedding was not going to be, they were going to come and see Sonja anyway.

Jim's family had already arrived in town, and all our family was there. Sonja was in very serious condition, so both families sent people to see her, two at a time, and stayed only a short time so as not to tire her.

Instead of the planned reception, my nieces and our kids enjoyed a celebration that she was alive by having a Chili party. It was a joyful occasion, because she hadn't died before she had gotten to the hospital, and that it happened before the wedding, instead of while they were on their planned Honeymoon in Hawaii. Her heart condition is so rare that doctors in Hawaii may not have been able to save her. We could only praise God that it happened when it did, if it had to happen. Jim never left the hospital for days. He was right by her side. I was thankful she had him.

The three-day celebration of the "wedding that wasn't" was over, so everyone returned home, leaving Sonja still in the hospital in a very scary predicament.

The clot hadn't dissolved, or even gotten one bit smaller, but the doctors were hoping that it would grab on to the side of the heart, so it couldn't move. After it was somewhat stabilized, she was released from the hospital, but was still at risk. She could rest at home as well as in the hospital, and take the drugs she needed.

We were on pins and needles, hoping the clot wouldn't move, and praying that it would dissolve. I knew how scared Bumper and I were and the fear Heidi, her brothers and poor Jim had. Just imagine the terror she was living in. She never showed one bit of fear. She was a rock!

THE SERIAL WEDDING

Jim and Sonja didn't want to get married in the hospital, as some of the doctors and nurses suggested. They were going to have a church wedding come hell or high water. When she was released, although still in a dangerous condition, they had a very small church wedding. She looked beautiful in her long gown.

The temperature in the church was freezing due to the fact they don't turn on a lot of heat except when something is going on, and a tiny wedding with only the bridal party, and Sonja's son Ari, did not account for anything big in the church.

The wedding took about five minutes, but it was nice, and we were glad it was short so Sonja wouldn't catch a cold on top of everything else.

They had a wedding dinner at a beautiful old mansion in St.Paul. We were in the attic, or what was the third floor. Sonja and Bumper took the elevators that were slow, and used mostly by the waiters. Once up, the place was delightful and expensive. By the place Jim had picked out, I knew he wasn't cheap, so that upped my opinion of him, which was already pretty high.

The bathrooms were located on the second floor, which meant we had to use that old elevator to go to them. The steps were winding and narrow, so I could have a problem if someone was coming up the steps, as we were going down, or vice versa. The restaurant was a quaint little spot, but if they had a fire, I think it could be difficult trying to get everyone out, but I'm sure they had a fire plan. If that would happen, Superman would come through the windows, or maybe trampolines were hidden under the windows for jumping. The place was nice, so I know they do have some system worked out. I just would have felt better had I known what it was.

It was an early evening wedding so Sonja wouldn't get tired, but a wonderful one! My daughter was now married to a man I felt would be perfect for her. I felt Jim was lucky for getting me for a mother-in-law!

THE BLOOD CLOT

The first part of January, Sonja had to go back to her doctor at the University Hospital. Two weeks before she was told, after a series of tests, that the blood clot was not any smaller, but was sticking to the heart. If the clot moved she could die. If it stuck to the wall, the situation wasn't good, but at least it would probably not move. They planned to cardiovert (electrically shock) her heart into a normal rhythm.

She was nervous going in for the tests, because she expected no change. I went with her, also in fear of the worst.

During tests to determine the status of the blood clot, several doctors came into the room looking rather stunned. She had the League of Nations in her room, because she had her own doctor, Dr. Wang, one doctor or fellow from Israel, one from Africa, and a third from someplace in Europe. They stood in silence while we were anxious about the bad report to come. Her doctor said, " IT'S GONE. IT CAN'T BE, BUT IT IS!" Each doctor was in a state of shock, because the medicines were not working, it hadn't shrunk in almost two months, and, all of a sudden, in one week, there was no sign of it. It could not have moved, or it would have gone to the lung, and she would be dead. "What happened?" were the words going around the room. The unanimous answer, "I don't know." Dr. Wang made a statement to the effect that something higher than the doctors had had a hand in this. I knew it was a miracle from God! They were then able to cardiovert her heart back to a normal beat.

We both rushed to phones to tell Jim and Bumper. Talking to Bumper, I could tell how happy he was, but I knew, without seeing him, that tears were falling from his happy eyes. I will bet Jim had tears in his eyes, too. A gift from God? Again? You can be sure of it!

THE SERIAL WEDDING RECEPTION

November 28, the wedding that wasn't, December 4th, the wedding that was. February 26, a reception was held at the University Club, overlooking the river in St. Paul.

Everyone invited to the wedding was there, except out-of-state relatives. The University Club was a beautiful, stately building on Summit Avenue, with many large windows facing downtown and the river. What a picturesque, serene and lovely view of the magical lights and the bridges. The clear snowy night made it look like a picture postcard.

Through the foyer was the bar, which had a breathtaking view of downtown. At the bar, was the first familiar face of the evening, my ex-husband, looking like he was perched for the night. Wandering though the bar, into the main room, we discovered more family members and friends. Heidi was again home from Wyoming, so this wedding created round-trip flights for her.

The setting was elegant, and the tables were beautifully decorated. Nothing could possibly go wrong now.

The photographer was there to take pictures of the bridal party in the clothes they had worn for the wedding. That should be simple enough!

The pictures were taken of the many families, which when a divorce has taken place, can be a lot of pictures. Bumper and me with all the kids, Jim's family with all their kids, and my ex wandered out of the bar for pictures of him and Maryanne with all the same kids that were in our picture.

The bride and groom were waiting, but the girls in the wedding party didn't show up. The photographer waited and waited. When patience ran out, he sent someone to look for them.

They were found changing clothes on the third floor, with one yet to get dressed. She was having a really big problem. She had come to the reception in old jeans, knowing she would change clothes and look beautiful shortly after arriving, not expecting anything to go wrong. A couple of the girls assessed the situation, and reported back to the photographer and the rest of us that there would be a very slight delay. " A few minutes?" the photographer said. " That shouldn't be a problem."

The few minutes turned into many minutes and tension began to set in. Even Bumper was getting concerned. I finally went up to see what the problem was, and there was Sonja's friend, Jane, trying to pull an unzipped dress over her body. The zipper was hopelessly stuck, and nothing they had tried would get it unstuck. Almost in tears, with little hope of wearing the dress, I had a quick solution. "Take it off, I know what to do. I ran down two flights of stairs, and enlightened the people as to what the problem was and asked Jon to fix it. He can fix anything! Mechanics are good at that! He took a look, tried it a few times, and broke the zipper wide open. " She can get it on now," he said.

Climbing up two flights of stairs in shock, I handed the dress to Jane and said, " I thought he could fix it."

At least she COULD get it over her head and on her body; the only problem was to make it stay together.

Having solved that problem, I didn't want to be involved anymore, so I just turned around, went through the door, down the stairs and decided the girls could figure it out themselves.

One girl went to the desk and made a plea for a lot of small pins, and after almost an hour, Jane came down looking beautiful, in a dress that fit perfectly. Several girls had toiled and slaved and put about a hundred little safety pins in the zipper, and not one pin showed. Those girls had talent!

The delay had changed the personality of the photographer. He seemed a little colder and more businesslike. He even looked different with his hair standing on end from his hands pulling on it. Bumper was a little testy, because the wonderful buffet assortment was delayed, and it was past feeding time at the Zoo. Ex-husband wasn't bothered at all, because the bar was open and free. He was one of only a few that was not frustrated by the delay.

Finally! Food! Good, Good Food~ A marvelous display of food! Bumper was in his glory. It didn't take him long to hit the table.

After dinner there was dancing with a DJ, and the cutting of the cake. Just when Jim got to the microphone to speak, a very special guest arrived. Sonja had invited Dr. Wang. It takes a rare occasion for a University doctor to come to a patient's wedding. She is a rare one, and also his pride and joy!

He was spotted trying to come in and sit quietly by himself in the back of the room. It didn't work! Jim stopped speaking and made the great doctor come forward, and he received a standing ovation from everyone in the room. With his entrance, there was hardly a dry eye in the crowd. He became the focal point with Sonja, because everyone wanted a picture of Sonja with her famous doctor. I think he was a little embarrassed, but I know he was proud and honored. He made a special occasion even MORE special.

The Serial wedding was almost ending, except for a honeymoon, which would not take place for about a year. Because Hawaii is a long way away, her doctor didn't want her that far from him for a good length of time. It would just be delayed like everything else connected to this wedding. No big deal! Sonja is alive and well! Sonja is a true miracle!

THE BALLS AND PARTIES

The years after Bumper's transplant were spent living the double life of grocery store employee to high society partygoers, my preference being the latter.

Hearst Castle Junior is like San Simeon in the many parties that are held in it. Bumper and I were excited about all the famous people, and like me, he started to believe that we belonged in the crowd we were in. It was harder for me when the pedestal fell, because he didn't have to go to work, so my fall was harder and higher.

The first time we met Howard Keel and his wife, Judy, at a party at Hearst Castle Junior, Howard sang for us. My favorite was Old Man River which I could remember him singing in a movie years before. Bumper and I knew the height of feeling important when you have a famous movie star singing to you in the privacy of someone's home, especially when that someone is a sister. Our life was so thrilling that I couldn't tell a lot of people back home about it, except my very best friends, because who would believe me?

"I went to a party in Palm Springs over the weekend, met George Montgomery, Howard Keel, and many more celebrities. Howard did a private show for us in my sister's living room." After looking at me like I belonged in the nut house, I could imagine that they would say," Sure you did, lady, I spent the weekend at the white house with the President." I had the brains to know that if I talked to people that I didn't know, customers in the store, I would be evaluated for commitment and maybe that would have been OK, because if I could prove my story, I would be sane!

Bumper always went at Thanksgiving, but sometimes, I would just fly in, because getting out was easier with one person traveling on a space available basis than with two people. We definitely are the World`s Poorest Jet Setters.

A few years ago, I sent Lori and Harvey a gift of two pheasants, bought from a game farm in Princeton, Minnesota. They shipped them to Palm Springs, and Lori loved the idea so much she decided to have a 'Dinner on the Farm' party.

She called and told me to send 12 more pheasants for this down home affair. I did that, and then decided I didn't want to miss it, so I called William to let him know there would be an extra pheasant, because there would be an extra guest. Great idea!

I did tell Lori I was coming just before the event, and she seemed to be happy, so I knew I was still loved. Bumper didn't want to go, so I went by myself.

The day before the party, I went with Lori out to Pegasus Riding Academy for the Handicapped, which is her riding school that teaches severely handicapped children and adults to ride horses. That is her love, and she has busloads coming every day during the winter months. Summer is too hot, so it is closed. After the riding, she decided we needed old boards and sagebrush for the 'Farm Dinner' décor the next night. She opened the truck of the Bentley and threw in some old lumber she found in the desert. Then she filled the rest of the trunk with sagebrush. When the trunk was full she opened the rear car doors and threw sagebrush and other desert refuse into the back seat of her beautiful car. I did help to some degree, but mostly, I was wondering if she is the one that needs to visit a shrink. "How in the world are you going to get this junk and all the little stickers cleaned off the car seats and trunk?" A reasonable question, I thought. " I'll have the gardener clean it." I bet that gardener loved her. It was a true mess and I can't believe anyone being able to get it cleaned up in a short time. Why would a gardener clean out a car? If you pay anyone extra money, I guess they would do it. Except me! If she had wanted or asked me to clean it, I wouldn't have had the foggiest idea of how to get those little burrs out, say nothing about all the dust and dirt that went with it.

As she was done loading the car with all that debris, she went to the barn and threw in a pitchfork, and shovel. We all know that pitchforks are used to put hay up for the horses, but I think I know what a shovel is for, and if I am correct, it is used to clean up what the other end of the horses drop. That went right in the trunk with the rest of the pile of junk. I would have been embarrassed to go through Palm Springs in some old rattletrap car, with tumbleweeds piled up to the roof of the back seat, but in a Bentley, it didn't seem so strange to me. I guess if you have a Bentley, you can be considered eccentric instead of nuts! Since I was in the car, I could be thought of as eccentric also! That made sense! Lori piled all the junk from the Bentley on the front entry of her house, and with her knack for decorating, it looked perfect! I could put the same stuff on a porch and it would look like a pile of garbage!

The guests all arrived in farm duds. Seeing Rosalie Hearst in a pair of jeans and denim shirt cracked me up, because that isn't the normal dress of the Rosalie I know and love. It was a down home atmosphere, and again, I had no problem of adapting to that lifestyle. But again, I had to face the reality of going home, back to work, and being careful about who I told of my true tales! My rear end often gets sore from falling off the pedestal of Glory!

Another time, when I flew in by myself, Lori told me that Kaye Ballard would be stopping by, but she didn't know when. "Kaye Ballard? I remember her." She was a popular singer in the 1950-60's and up. I was excited about her coming. William had to go to the grocery store. Harvey was in his study, and Lori was at the other end of the house in her den when the doorbell rang. William always answers the front door, but William was gone. Harvey and Lori didn't know he was gone and they don't normally answer the door.

What should I do? I was contemplating my choices, which were only two, answer the door, or not answer the door. What if it was a kidnapper? I could tell him I was the only one home and he wouldn't want me. What if it was Kaye Ballard? What would I say? I decided my only choice was to go to the door dressed as I was in my back home around the house attire.

I opened the door, and Kaye Ballard looked exactly as she did as I remember her when I was young! I was old, but she was still young! I could have picked her out anyplace, in a minute.

Seeing her in person took me by surprise, although I knew at some point she was expected. I was alone this time, no Lori or Harvey to untie my tongue. I looked at her and shouted," Kaye Ballard." Then I grabbed her and gave her a hug. She was more surprised to see me than I was to see her. I knew she was nice when she hugged me back, and then said, "Am I keeping you from cooking?" At that I burst out laughing and told her that I was Lori's sister, and William was at the store. She started laughing also, so the ice was broken. I asked if I could take her jacket, since it was a warm day. She said, "I like to leave it on, it covers my fat." A woman after my own heart! I loved her then. We have the same problem! Anyone that hugs the unknown help cannot be bad!

On a different trip to Palm Springs, Harvey and Lori took his mother, Stanley and Maryanne, Bumper and me to a beautiful country club for lunch, where Kirk Douglas sold and signed his books. After buying the books and having them signed, I went to the ladies' room and stood right next to Mrs. Douglas (Anne) when I washed my hands. That was even an honor. In my sister's circles, it wouldn't be, but I was an outsider looking in, and becoming a good actress.

Bumper and I have had the honor of meeting Ginger Rogers, Magda Gabor, Florence Henderson, Sidney Sheldon, Johnny Mann (of the Johnny Mann singers), Mousie Powell (widow of William

Powell), Harry Guardino, Pactrick McNee, Francis Lederer and W.P. Kinsella, who is the author of "Shoeless Joe", which became the movie "Field of Dreams". I have been hugged by Art Newman, who is the brother of Paul Newman and also his look-a-like. We have had the joy of meeting many famous and wonderful people.

Oh the Palm Springs events, how I love them!

THE END OF AN ERA

After being sick for many months, Rosalie Hearst died in October, 1999. She was the sweetest, most down to earth woman I have had the pleasure of meeting. She made Bumper and me feel special, although she knew many famous and powerful people. Each time I saw her, before I left for home, she would give me a kiss and say, "I love you." She let her friends know that she loved them, and I think that is something that should be done more often, by everyone.

From Rosalie, I learned that the very wealthy are some of the kindest people I know. She had a saying that I will always remember, "It is nice to be important, but more important to be nice." That was Rosalie Hearst.

Rosalie's Memorial Service in Palm Springs was a wonderful affair, just the way she wanted it. The service was in church, but the reception afterwards was at Lori and Harvey's 'Hearst Castle Junior', because it had been Rosalie's home at one time.

She wanted her favorite food served, since it was her party, although she would not be able to attend. Her wish was to have fried chicken, a hot dog stand, tamale pie, ice cream wagon, and a full bar.

Bumper and I were honored, because we received invitations for the event. Bumper couldn't make it, but I went with Lori and Harvey.

I thought I knew Rosalie, but was soon to know more about her when friends talked about her during the service. She was remarkably funny!

I think Rosalie would have loved watching dignitaries, the Hearst family, known dress designers, millionaires, and a grocery store peon eating the wonderful food she so loved. By watching the crowd, I had to believe the menu was a shock to some of them.

A part of Palm Springs died with Rosalie, and I don't think the town will ever be quite the same.

She treated all people with dignity and respect, and she made me feel like I was a very special person.

Bumper and I will always have a place in our hearts for this wonderful woman, and are privileged for the joy of knowing her for ten years.

TRAVELING THE WORLD

The family gatherings at Thanksgiving have always been a time of love, fun and excitement. One of the most exciting things is to find out where our travels will take us the next summer.

Harvey sends his brother Stanley, wife Maryanne, Bumper and me on a trip somewhere in the world every year. The excitement builds as Thanksgiving nears, as to where we will go!

We have been to the French Riviera, Rome and Barcelona on cruises. We've seen the monkeys on top of Gibraltar and walked through the open fish market in Casablanca. We've seen Lisbon, Portugal with its beautiful seaport, where the statue can be seen for miles. We have been fortunate to see the Beaches of Normandy, and the British Isles. We've seen Mt. Fuji and ridden the bullet train in Tokyo, and seen The Great Wall of China. In the Forbidden City a crowd of nearly 100 Chinese people followed Bumper around. I was mad. I didn't know why they were always following him and wanting to take his picture. Later, we found out that some idiot had started a rumor that he was Colonel Sanders. In Beijing, there is a statue of the famous man outside the KFC, in the same type of clothes Bumper was wearing, and Bumper has the same kind of beard. The statue also makes Colonel Sanders look heavy like Bumper. He was famous!

We have seen the Terracotta soldiers in Xion, China. Gone down the Li River and were offered Snake wine from a large cask of wine with larger snakes floating around in it. The snakes were dead, but we all thought we would be, too, if we drank it.

We've been to Israel, Hong Kong (before it went back to China), and the Pyramids. We've spent seven days on the Nile River, and have toured Cairo. Each time we travel, we are happy to have seen that part of the world, but thankful to be back in the U.S. where we have everything that is either a luxury or non-existent in that part of the world. We take good doctors for granted, as some places have none. Our Egypt pamphlet states that once you leave Luxor, the doctors that do exist have unknown qualifications, meaning, no degrees in anything!

We have traveled by bus through Eastern Europe, starting at Vienna, going to Budapest, Poland, and the death camps, Warsaw, Berlin, Prague, and back to Vienna, a trip through history that should never be forgotten.

Bumper may have been in more foreign countries than any other heart transplant person, but it is not proven. Many of them would choose not to go where the medical situation is so uncertain, but we have loved the challenge, although it was sometimes scary for us. He has gotten sick in foreign countries, but we have done it and made it home safely.

We are blessed with relatives that care enough to send us to all the foreign countries we have seen. After each trip, we are thankful we live in a country of freedom and good medical care. We are blessed with having the title of the World's Poorest Jet Setters, and fitting into an alien lifestyle of the rich and famous, treading on ground where we do not belong, but love to be.

Not many people have had the wonderful experiences and travels that we are fortunate enough to have had.

We are also blessed with having four children that love us, and seven healthy grandchildren.

Yes, there is a God.

Oh yes, 1999 Heidi shot a very, VERY, large Buffalo in Wyoming, and will be in "BOON And CROCKET", which is the WHO'S WHO of hunting.